French Bread Baking Made Easy

Nida .H Bender

Funny helpful tips:

Invest in experiences over material possessions; memories last a lifetime.

Prioritize debt management; a healthy balance sheet attracts investors and partners.

French Bread Baking Made Easy : Master the Art of French Bread Baking: A Step-by-Step Guide to Perfect Loaves Every Time.

<u>Life advices:</u>

Seek mutual respect; it's the cornerstone of a healthy relationship.

Establish boundaries; they protect the sanctity of the relationship.

Introduction

This book invites you on a delightful journey into the art of crafting classic French bread. From understanding the essential ingredients and tools to mastering step-by-step techniques, this cookbook is your guide to achieving crusty, delicate, round, chewy, buttery, and airy French bread creations.

The journey begins with a comprehensive exploration of the ingredients and tools needed to embark on your French bread baking adventure. The step-by-step instructions that follow ensure that even beginners can confidently produce authentic French bread. The cookbook goes the extra mile by addressing the challenges of baking at high altitudes, providing valuable insights for achieving success in various environments.

About the recipes, the cookbook introduces you to a diverse range of French bread styles, each meticulously crafted to capture the essence of French baking. From the crusty and delicate to the round and chewy, and finally, the buttery and airy, you'll find a recipe to suit every taste and occasion.

For those eager to go beyond traditional bread, "French Bread Baking Cookbook for Beginners" offers a tantalizing section titled "Beyond Bread." This section explores creative ways to use French bread in other culinary delights, expanding the possibilities for your culinary repertoire.

To ensure ease of use, the cookbook includes measurement conversions, making it accessible to a global audience. Whether you're a novice or a seasoned baker, this cookbook equips you with the knowledge and practical guidance needed to master the art of French bread baking.

Get ready to fill your kitchen with the irresistible aroma of freshly baked French bread, as you unlock the secrets of this timeless culinary tradition.

Contents

CHAPTER 1

FRENCH BREAD 101

If bread is life, French bread is la belle vie (the good life!). French loaves have an undeniable quality, finesse, and artistry about them, and in this chapter, we'll discuss just what, exactly, makes French bread so special. Get ready to embark on your breadmaking journey, during which we'll focus on kneading, fermentation, shaping, proofing, and baking a variety of breads. We'll also talk about the tools and ingredients you'll need to get started, as well as the terms and techniques that you'll soon be using.

CLASSIC FRENCH BREAD

Humans have been making bread for centuries, but with the popularization of artisan loaves, most of us have gotten used to picking up fantastic bread from our local bakery or even the supermarket instead of baking it ourselves. Why take on such a challenge when you can pick up a gorgeous, crusty loaf for just a few dollars? The truth is that, although it's wonderful to support the professional bakers doing amazing things with bread, it can't quite compare to the experience of baking your own. The satisfaction of pulling a homemade loaf out of your oven and knowing that you, with your own hands, made it happen . . . well, there's just nothing better.

  If you've visited a boulangerie or your local bakeshop, you've no doubt seen rows and rows of unique breads and viennoiseries lining the shelves, not to mention glamorous tarts and cakes. Each shop is like a jewel box, with items glistening as they're loaded onto shelves and into baskets early in the morning. Well, what if I told you that you didn't have to leave your house to have these, and that you could be biting into your very own bread tomorrow morning?

With just a few ingredients and a little know-how, you, too, can create magic in your kitchen. I know it can seem daunting, but the recipes in this book are formulated with the idea of keeping things simple. Can you lengthen your fermentation time? Absolutely. Can you play with different blends of flours and levels of hydration in some of those more rustic breads? Of course. But this book is designed to get you started with fail-safe instructions for classic loaves, to take an idea that may seem intimidating and turn it into something uncomplicated. Everyone should experience the satisfaction of cutting into a loaf of bread they bake, whether it's once a day or once a month, and this book will help get you there.

What makes French bread unique?

Is there anything more symbolic of French culture than golden baguettes slung over shoulders? When I was my way to Paris for the first time, there was nothing I looked forward to more than my first trip to a boulangerie, when I'd finally get to have one of those coveted loaves for myself. Would I ask for it bien cuit (well-cooked) or pas trop cuit (not too cooked)? Oh, the dilemma!

Whether slathered with jam, filled with meats and cheeses, or transformed into pain perdu or exquisitely crafted tartines, French breads have rightly earned their reputation as the finest in the world. They are expertly crafted and baked, with the touch and understanding that only generations of bakers toiling at their craft can obtain. Each loaf is informed by the baker's artistic preferences and traditions that have spanned centuries. And because there is access to fantastic bread everywhere in France, the standard is high. There are even laws defining what ingredients may be included in each kind of bread—for instance, in a baguette, only flour, water, salt, and leavening may be used, and it must weigh between 250 and 300 grams and measure in at 55 to 65 centimeters. There are also no preservatives or additives; because of this, people sometimes purchase bread multiple times a day so that it is freshly baked for each meal.

Baking is also serious business. More than 70 percent of the nation's bread is still meticulously produced in boulangeries by hand, and competitions such as the Grand Prix de la Baguette de la Ville de Paris leave bakers to vie for the title of Best Baguette in Paris. You can just imagine what a glorious time that is.

La Cordelette
1,10 €

La Bastidette
1,00 €

Ficelle
0,95 €

Types and shapes of French bread

A defining feature of French breads is their variety of lovely shapes. In this book, you'll learn about all types of French breads: the fluffy, tender loaves of brioche and pain de mie; the chewy, deeply flavored boules; the light, flaky croissants; and, of course, the iconic baguette. And while you're learning to bake them, you'll also learn about their iconic shapes.

I've designed these recipes to give you the simplest introduction possible to the techniques French bakers use for shaping their loaves. I want you to not only enjoy the final product but also enjoy the process.

We'll look at how to pre-shape dough to facilitate the later shaping process—turning a mass of dough into rounds or rectangles that then turn into long baguettes, expertly shaped boules (balls), bâtards (footballs), or couronnes (rings). You'll learn to manipulate dough to achieve the shape that you want while protecting the delicate composition of the loaf's internal structure.

You'll also learn about ways of scoring and cutting dough to transform a standard loaf into one with a signature design, such as pain d'épi, fougasse, pain brié, and viennoise au chocolat. We'll also touch on how you can use a stencil to achieve an impressive result with minimal effort.

These final flourishes are what elevate French bread from being just incredibly delicious foods to works of art.

Crust and crumb

If you ever go on social media, you'll no doubt have seen beautiful cross sections of dough and videos of bakers slicing their loaves or viennoiseries in half to show off their internal structures. French breads offer a variety of different textures, from the gaping, open holes in baguettes to the tight, tender crumb of pain de mie. In the recipes that follow, you'll see how high-hydration doughs bake up into loaves with deeply colored crusts and open interiors, whereas chewy loaves may be easier to work by hand and will be a bit denser. Each of these textures has its own merits; those hearty, open loaves soften wonderfully when they sop up a plate of sauce and are exquisite slathered with butter that melts into those open crevices. Slightly denser loaves make for perfect sandwiches or Tartines. Brioche, le cramique, and other enriched breads are lovely as an accompaniment to un café au lait for breakfast and can also be the base for other sweet recipes, such as Pain Perdu with Whipped Crème Fraîche.

We'll also take a brief look at lamination. This highly satisfying (although somewhat lengthy) undertaking will reward you with croissants made with layers of rolled-in butter.

Bread-Baking Terms

bench: Your countertop; a clean surface on which you can work with dough

crumb: The interior structure of bread, often described as "tight" for more even structures, or "open" for breads with large, more irregular pockets

elasticity: A dough's ability to spring back when stretched

extensibility: The ability of a dough to be stretched

fermentation: When yeast digests sugars in flour and converts them to carbon dioxide, which becomes trapped by the gluten structure in dough, causing bread to rise and giving it texture and flavor

folding: A process of gently folding dough to enhance the internal structure

gluten: Proteins found in wheat (glutenin and gliadin) that give bread its structure by trapping gases during fermentation

hydration: The ratio of liquid to flour by weight in a recipe

kneading: The process of mixing and working dough by hand or with a mixer to develop gluten

levain: The "leaven" (also known as sourdough starter or la mère, "mother dough"); a living ferment made by cultivating wild yeasts and bacteria through a mixture of flour and water to give dough rise (without commercial yeast)

oven spring: The increase in volume of dough in the oven during the initial bake time

pâte fermentée: A preferment made with flour, yeast, water, and salt; typically a bit of dough saved from the previous day

poolish: A preferment made of equal parts flour and water mixed with yeast in a low quantity

preferment: The portion of a dough made ahead and added to the final mix of dough to improve flavor and texture; levain, poolish, pâte fermentée, and sponges are all preferments

proof: The final rise before baking

seam: The line indicating where a loaf has been folded or shaped; also cle ("key") in French

sponge: A quick preferment made to help activate low-hydration doughs or enriched doughs

windowpane test: The ability to stretch a small piece of dough thin enough for light to pass through

GETTING STARTED WITH INGREDIENTS AND TOOLS

The best part of breadmaking is that you typically need only a few key ingredients and a few special tools to get started. I've included instructions for mixing recipes by hand, so if you don't have a stand mixer, don't worry. I also offer information about different styles of authentic French flours, so you can incorporate them into your breads, if you'd like.

Ingredients

You may need only a few ingredients to create wonderful loaves, but the flavor can be enhanced by choosing those ingredients carefully.

Flour: The best flour for breadmaking is a high-quality flour without whitening properties. In the United States, we categorize flour by protein content: Bread flour typically has 12 to 13 percent gluten, whereas all-purpose flour is slightly lower at 10 to 12 percent. King Arthur Flour and Bob's Red Mill make very high-quality flour.

In France, flours are categorized by mineral content. You'll see notes in this book for T150, T55, and so on (provided as an alternative to American-style flours). Lower T numbers are lighter in color and have a finer texture and a high protein content, whereas higher T numbers have a bit more graininess and color and lower levels of gluten. They're also more flavorful, due to the increased quantity of bran (the outer portion of the wheat berry). You may be able to find French flours in specialty shops in your area, or you can purchase them online.

Water: The type of water you use can affect your bread. Generally, tap or filtered water is perfect. But if you wouldn't be comfortable drinking a glass of your tap water, substitute bottled water at room temperature.

The temperature of the water can also make a big difference. Warm water will speed up fermentation, cold water will slow it down, and hot water will kill yeast. (See French Bread FAQ and Troubleshooting Guide for more details.)

Yeast: There are three main types of commercial yeast: instant, active dry, and fresh. No one type is better than another. Traditionally, active dry yeast needed to be "proofed" or "proved" in a liquid before being used, but due to manufacturing changes, all types of yeast can now be added to the mix in the same way. But yeasts are not interchangeable. In the recipes in this book, I use instant yeast, but if you have another type, follow this simple conversion: 1 part instant yeast = 1½ parts active yeast = 3 parts fresh yeast. Store active dry and instant yeasts in the freezer for the longest shelf life, and fresh yeast well wrapped in the refrigerator.

Instant and active dry yeasts are shelf stable with long shelf lives. SAF yeast, made in France, is a popular brand; SAF Red is their instant, and SAF Gold is their osmotolerant variety. (Osmotolerant yeast requires less liquid to work and is made for dough recipes that contain lots of sugar—sugar steals the moisture yeast needs to survive.) If you're able to locate fresh yeast, give it a try, although it does have a shorter life span of only about two weeks in the refrigerator.

Salt: I use kosher salt in these recipes. Avoid iodized salt or salt that's too fine (you may end up adding more salt than intended).

Sugar: The recipes in this book use granulated sugar. Once you're comfortable with these recipes, you can try using other sweeteners, such as honey or agave syrup.

Butter: European-style butter contains a higher level of fat than American butter (typically as high as 86 percent). Because these types of butter contain less water, they take longer to melt and are easier to work with. For breads with laminated doughs, such as croissants, I recommend looking for European high-fat butters, which impart a flakier texture.

Eggs: The protein in eggs promotes a tender, rich crumb. Eggs from pastured chickens can subtly enhance bread's flavor.

Milk: These recipes are designed with whole-fat cow's milk, but you can also try them with nondairy milks. Soy, oat, rice, and nut milks impart a bit of their own flavor characteristics.

Chocolate: I use both dark and milk chocolate depending on my mood, but the key is to use a type that you would want to snack on (preferably with the percentage of cacao on the label).

Must-have equipment

When making bread, you don't actually need very much equipment. Here is a list of all the items you'll need to make the recipes in this book. I've tried to keep this list as short as possible, but I really do recommend having all these items on hand.

Bench scrapers: A plastic bench scraper is perfect for gently scooping doughs out of bowls and onto your bench, as well as scraping up dough to move it around and removing excess flour from your surface. A metal bench scraper is great for portioning doughs. In a pinch, a chef's knife can handle portioning as well.

Bowls: You should have at least a couple of medium stainless steel or glass bowls for mixing and fermenting doughs (or a stand mixer).

Cooling racks: These are necessary to ensure breads cool evenly, without any soggy bottoms.

Heavy baking sheets: These are essential. The heavier the weight, the more evenly breads will brown (because their bottoms will be protected).

Linen towels: For certain recipes, you may be able to use plastic wrap for covering dough. But lint-free linen dish towels are great for covering dough, lining proofing vessels, or creating folds to house loaves while proofing. An alternative is a baker's couche, an untreated, unbleached, 100 percent flax linen cloth used by professional bakers. (If you can't find linen towels, you can use cotton kitchen towels; just make sure they are also lint-free.)

Loaf pans: In this book, we use loaf pans for brioche and pain de mie. A standard 9-by-5-inch loaf pan is perfect, although if you fall in love with pain de mie, you might want to invest in a Pullman loaf for that classic square shape (the top of the pan prevents the bread from doming in the oven).

Oven mitts: These are essential for handling hot trays and transferring hot loaves onto cooling racks.

Parchment paper: I buy packs of precut parchment paper sheets, perfectly sized for my baking sheets. Parchment paper is essential for good baking and also for easy cleanup. In this book we also use it to help move breads into a hot Dutch oven or onto a baking stone.

Pastry brush: This is used for dusting off excess flour, egg washing, or greasing pans. Any standard brush will do, although you should avoid brushes that frequently lose their bristles. Look for a brush light enough in texture that it won't deflate your loaves if you add glaze after proofing (I avoid silicone brushes for this reason).

Rolling pin: This is handy for rolling dough, but a clean wine bottle can work in a pinch.

Spray bottle: These are great for spraying loaves during the first phase of baking to delay crust formation and create steam. If you can't get a spray bottle in time, put a cake pan or cast-iron skillet on the bottom rack of your oven while preheating, and pour about an inch of boiling water in it after the loaves are put into the oven, to create a steamy environment.

Nice-to-have equipment

Bread has been made by hand for thousands of years, and I still prefer this method. That being said, there is some equipment (other than the essentials I've listed) you can use to make your work easier. This list includes a stand mixer, which will take some time off the process—and some pressure off your shoulders.

Baking stone: A preheated baking stone creates a hot surface for the bottom of the loaf to rest on, ensuring a crisp, evenly browned bottom.

Bannetons (proofing baskets): These handy vessels support the shape and structure of dough during proofing; the unlined baskets can also give a unique, spiraled look to your loaves. A bowl or colander lined with a generously floured linen towel can also do the job.

Digital scale: In this book, recipes are written using two units of measure: volume and weight. In the beginning, you can use those cups and tablespoons you have on hand. But to really measure ingredients precisely and to scale out dough for consistent sizing, I definitely recommend a kitchen scale.

Dutch oven (cocotte): A Dutch oven, called a cocotte in France, is a heavy pot typically made of enameled cast iron, with a tight-fitting lid. If you make the same loaf of bread twice, and bake one in a Dutch oven and one on a baking stone, I really believe you'll have better results with the former. Think of it like an oven within your oven. Dutch ovens retain heat, and once the loaf goes in and the lid goes on, the bread steams itself. This keeps the crust flexible during the initial oven spring, which means the bread will have a more voluminous and impressive internal structure.

Lame or razor: A lame is a curved blade used for scoring bread dough before baking. You can use a straight razor or a clean single-edge razor instead; either offers a fun way to give each loaf a unique flourish.

Stand mixer with dough hook: A stand mixer can really take some of the work out of the bread-making process and give you the opportunity to make multiple and larger batches.

Thermometer: If you're in doubt about whether your loaf has finished baking, checking the internal temperature can be a great way to set your mind at ease.

Wooden peel: This is useful for transferring loaves to a hot stone in the oven, but you can also slide the loaf onto a stone using parchment paper.

Measuring Ingredients and Using a Digital Scale

For those of us just starting out with breadmaking, a scale is crucial. There's nothing worse than pulling your bread out of the oven and knowing something is wrong but not knowing why. Inaccurate measurements are often the culprit. The recipes in this book include measurements by volume, but you'll find that weighing the ingredients in grams can remove a lot of guesswork.

When using a scale, put the bowl or measuring cup on top of the scale and press "tare" to zero out the weight. Then you'll able to start at zero and measure each ingredient without having to do any math. For accurate weights, make sure to press "tare" after each ingredient is added.

If measuring with dry cup measures, be sure to spoon and level for accurate results. To do this, spoon the dry ingredient into the measuring cup, then use the flat side of a knife to scrape over the top to eliminate any excess. (Scooping flour directly from the bag will pack the flour down, making it dense, and you'll end up with more than you need.)

STEP-BY-STEP FRENCH BREAD

Although French doughs are unique in flavor and shape, the breadmaking process is quite simple. It's a matter of attuning yourself to knowing what to look for as your environment changes (the temperature or humidity of the season, for example), and that takes practice. But you will find that you use the same steps time and time again.

Breadmaking is a sensory experience. As you mix and knead dough, you'll begin to notice texture. Is the dough smooth? Does it have a good stretch? Is it supple? The recipes will give you cues to look for to determine if you've developed enough gluten to move on to fermentation. And once you're happy with that structure, you and your dough get to take a rest. Your first round of fermentation can take as little as 1 hour, or as long as 24. Some of that is up to you, but some of it is regulated by what type of dough you're making. (We'll talk about what to look for in each recipe.)

After fermentation, not only has the texture of the dough transformed, but the aroma has, as well. You can begin to sense the final product. And then comes the fun part: shaping. The more practice you get with portioning and shaping dough, the more expert and gentle your shaping will be, leading to a more open crumb in your bread. After a little while, you'll effortlessly rotate the dough into perfect rounds, cupping one side in each hand as you turn and tighten. Your hands will work quickly without needing your brain to direct them.

And then we rest again. There's one final proof before baking, the last chance for the dough to increase in volume at room temperature, which will determine the size and crumb structure of your loaf. Oven spring will do some work as well, as the bread will increase in size up to 30 percent when it first goes into the oven. And baking your bread until it is a deep golden brown will give you the ideal deep crust and tender interior.

Combining

Depending on the recipe, and whether or not you use a preferment (see here), combining the ingredients can sometimes be quite simple: All the ingredients go into a bowl, you give them a quick mix to combine (with a wooden spoon, your hands, or a mixer), and there you have it! This is called frasage—a rough mix of the ingredients that forms a shaggy mass. As soon as a liquid and flour are combined, they instantly begin to form bonds of gluten. (To develop these strands into a more complex and organized structure, we knead the dough; more on that to come.)

When using a preferment, you're adding a step to the process I've just described: You mix a doughlike substance that can vary in consistency, depending on the hydration level, then set it aside to develop gluten and build flavor. This then gets mixed with the remaining ingredients in the dough recipe to create that same shaggy mass.

DOES INGREDIENT ORDER MATTER?

Ingredient order definitely matters. Salt is hygroscopic (as is sugar), meaning it captures the moisture that yeast needs to survive, thereby dehydrating the yeast. For this reason, I always add salt on top of the dry ingredients, and then mix. I also like to put the wet ingredients and yeast in the bowl first, to eliminate any possibility of granules of yeast hanging around after the initial mix, or flour sticking to the bottom of the bowl. When using a preferment, I also add the liquid ingredients to the preferment first, loosening it, and then add the rest of the ingredients.

TEMPERATURE

Just as ingredient order can matter, ingredient temperature can also play an important role in baking. Imagine that you're mixing a supple brioche dough, adding thick pats of butter. Let's say your kitchen is warm (it's the middle of July) and so your butter is very soft. That fat will soften the dough and create a sticky mess that will be difficult to shape. A good way to solve this issue is by chilling the dough before shaping; another option is to note the temperature of your environment and adjust the temperature of your ingredients accordingly. In the middle of winter, for example, you may want to work with liquids that are slightly warmed to help kick-start yeast activity. (Note that your water should never go above 120°F, at which point yeast will begin to die.) But just as using warm liquid can help kick-start fermentation, using cool liquid in warm weather can slow things down, ensuring that the dough will not accidentally over-proof.

Knead it or not

As we've seen in recent years with the popularity of no-knead breadmaking, kneading is not a requirement for making good bread. No-knead breadmaking replaces the intensity of kneading with lengthened fermentation times, letting bread build its own gluten structure as the yeast converts sugars to carbon dioxide and the dough stretches. Freaky, right?

In this book, however, we work with classic doughs that are made by hand. You're going to feel the dough structure develop as you knead; you'll use your fingers to test for proper fermentation; and you'll move, shape, and, finally, score the dough before it ultimately bakes into its final form.

I love my stand mixer, and I use it to whip up all types of items, but when we talk about the art of breadmaking, the soul that each loaf contains, I don't believe that the process is really complete if you don't use your hands.

Here's how you do it: Put the dough on your bench, push it away from you with your palm, bring it back toward you. Repeat. You'll see the dough transform and become smooth, supple, and stretchy by the time you've finished working with it. Higher levels of hydration mean stickier doughs. I've known plenty of bakers who don't like having dough stick to their hands, but for these types of dough, there's just no way around it. Lean into the stickiness! Slap the dough against your bench, pushing it away from you and back again, working it over and over until the stickiness subsides as gluten develops. (A bench scraper is essential for these types of sticky dough; it scrapes up the dough as you work it.)

Don't be tempted to add flour. Often, when rolling out pie dough, for example (and in this book, croissants), you need to flour your bench to ensure that the dough will not stick. With bread doughs, if you dust your bench with flour, that flour gets absorbed by the dough, changing the recipe. The quantity of flour in your dough increases, and you'll be left with a heavier product. Instead of adding flour, knead more. Remember that the more you knead, the less sticky the dough will become.

Folding dough involves a slightly different process. As with other methods, you combine the ingredients and set them aside to ferment, but, instead of using a lengthy kneading process and then setting the dough aside, you occasionally visit the dough during fermentation. You wet your hands to avoid sticking, and you stretch and fold the dough in the bowl three or four times before setting it aside again. This process enhances the structure of the dough, just as kneading does, but is perfect for doughs with very high levels of hydration, which tend to be a bit too difficult to knead by hand. Typically, this also means you'll need a longer fermentation time; the time between folds can vary depending on the recipe.

For future breadmaking projects, you can combine these methods: A no-knead bread with a few folds can have a bit more structure and still give you ease of production.

There's no right or wrong method when it comes to baking bread. The most important thing is finding the method that works for you as you develop your technique.

First rise: bulk fermentation

We've kneaded the dough and set it aside. Now the first round of fermentation starts. (The term "bulk fermentation" applies to doughs that will be divided and shaped into multiple loaves or buns.) In this stage, yeast gets working to convert carbohydrates into carbon dioxide, which becomes trapped by the newly formed network of gluten, creating lift and giving the bread texture and flavor. The optimal temperature range for this stage is 75°F to 80°F; warmer or cooler temperatures will either slow or quicken this process.

Cold fermentation will slow the process and give us more control over when we bake the bread; for instance, a fermentation for 1 to 2 hours at room temperature could be extended to overnight in the refrigerator. This slower fermentation also creates a more developed flavor and structure.

As gases are produced and retained in the gluten network's structure, dough swells. (This is what causes the "rise.") You'll notice that, in most recipes, you're looking for the dough to increase in volume by a specific amount before you go on to the next step. It can be helpful to take a photo of the dough before and after bulk fermentation, to compare and see the increase in size (this can vary depending on the type of dough). For high-hydration doughs, you'll also see large air pockets along the sides of the container (if your container is clear).

As the gluten is stretched by this rise, the dough's strength increases. After fermentation, the dough should have an increase in extensibility (how much the dough can be stretched). This is when a windowpane test (see here) can be useful. If you find that your dough is a bit tight or hasn't increased in volume as called for in the recipe, give the rise more time. Remember that temperature can play a role in slowing fermentation, and often the temperature and humidity in your kitchen may be changing the rate of your dough's rise more than you realize.

Sometimes, beginning bakers who are in a hurry will skip this first rise, thinking that their final proof will disguise their haste. But the first rise not only improves the flavor of the dough but also relaxes it for shaping. If you don't rest the dough after you've kneaded it, shaping becomes more difficult. You will notice the dough shrinking back, fighting you as you work it. If you're worried about time, try controlling the temperature of your environment for fermentation (and therefore the time it takes to rise) to make the timing of the dough work for your schedule. Using the refrigerator to slow things down is always a good option.

Pre-shaping and shaping

The dough has rested and risen; now it's time to portion and shape. (Don't forget that although it's tempting to generously flour your bench during this stage, adding additional flour will ruin the texture of your final loaf. Lightly flouring is the way to go.)

When it comes to portioning, a metal bench scraper is a great tool, though a good chef's knife will work as well. You don't want to hack away at the dough, accidentally tightening the gluten structure as you portion and bursting large pockets of air that you may want to show up in the final product (depending on the type of bread). Instead, estimate as best as you can with each cut. For example: If you're dividing the dough in two, mark the dough in the center as best as you can, make one clean cut, and weigh for consistency. If needed, you can take a piece from here or there to even things out.

Once you've portioned the dough, you'll form each piece into a rough shape, guiding it toward the final shape that you want. For example, to shape a baguette, you'll start by pre-shaping the sections of dough into rough rounds, with the seams on the bottom. You'll do this by pulling the edges of the dough toward the center, repeating until you're satisfied with the shape, and pinching the seam to seal (see here for photos and more detailed instructions).

After pre-shaping, leave the pieces of dough on your bench, covered (with a towel or plastic wrap) to prevent a skin from forming, and allow them to rest. You've worked the gluten a bit, and that gluten needs to relax again. This could take from 5 to 30 minutes, depending on the recipe.

Once they've rested, the pre-shaped loaves shouldn't offer too much resistance, and you should be able to guide them into their final shape. Each kind of French bread has its own shape, and each recipe will have specific directions about how to achieve that shape. Keep in mind that doughs can be shaped in myriad ways. For example, a lean dough used for baguettes can be turned into pain d'épi (which resembles a stalk of wheat), pain couronne (a crown), and more.

You want to be somewhat gentle with doughs that are intended to have an open crumb, such as baguettes, boule de pain, or pain de campagne. Those large pockets of gas are important for the texture of the final loaf, and if you destroy them now, you'll only get smaller pockets during the final rise. Make sure the seam (the line indicating where a loaf has been folded or shaped) is at the bottom of the loaf (unless you're using a proofing basket, in which case it should be faceup because the loaf will be flipped before baking) before setting the dough aside for its final proof.

Second rise

During pre-shaping and shaping, we degassed the dough a bit. Notice how the large gas bubbles that were once making up the majority of the dough have now somewhat subsided. In some doughs, you may even have pushed them out intentionally. Now we'll give the yeast a final chance to continue its work of creating carbon dioxide. This expansion during the final proof sets the tone for the bread's final volume.

In this stage, it's essential to keep temperature in mind. The same temperature rules apply that applied during bulk fermentation, namely that a room that is too cool or too warm will affect the rate of fermentation. You also want to be especially careful when proofing enriched or laminated doughs, because a final proof in an environment that is too warm could cause some fat to leach out of the dough, ruining the flaky layers you've created (in the case of croissants, for example).

I like to use the "poke test" to determine whether my bread has fully proofed. Here's how to do it: Give the loaf a poke in an inconspicuous area (where it won't ruin the shape). It should feel marshmallow-y—soft, but solid—and light, and your finger should leave a bit of an indent. If the dough springs back all the way and feels very firm to the touch, give it more time. Conversely, if it looks on the verge of deflation, or that poking it could make it pop like a balloon, you may have over-proofed the dough. Keeping an eye on the dough and checking it occasionally during fermentation can help prevent over-proofing, but if you do forget your dough, don't worry! Typically, you can degas the loaf, shape it again, and proof again (for a shorter time) before baking. If you need to do this, follow the same instructions as before, but this time, test the dough every 10 minutes or so as it rises. Whatever you do, please don't throw the dough away. Although it may not bake into the perfect bread, it will still be absolutely delicious.

Designs and finishes

Once the loaf has risen, it's time to finish up the design. If the bread requires an egg wash, do this very gently with a pastry brush, to avoid deflating the loaves. Egg wash will help create even browning and give your breads a beautiful sheen.

If you're scoring a design into the loaf, you can use a lame, razor, or even kitchen shears to create a decorative pattern or shape. Scoring doesn't just give your loaf an artisanal look, it also helps the dough expand during baking and release gas without splitting the crust. Take care to be gentle but decisive while scoring, and aim for about ¼-inch-deep cuts, unless the recipe specifies otherwise. If your dough is under-proofed, you'll need to slash a bit deeper, because the bread will expand more during the initial bake. Or, if the dough isn't ready, just wait longer before scoring! (In the pain brié recipe, where deeper cuts are required, you'll see a note that reminds you to be careful about your proof time for this reason.) Conversely, if your dough has over-proofed before you attempt to score it, you'll need an extra-careful hand to avoid deflating it.

The bake

We're ready to bake!

Your oven should be preheated until it reaches the temperature called for in the recipe. Ideally the oven should preheat while the bread is proofing so it will be ready to go as soon as the bread is.

Check each recipe for notes about using a Dutch oven, baking sheet, or baking stone; with the exception of the Dutch oven, which may need more space, all baking should be done on the center rack of the oven.

If you follow bakers on social media, you no doubt have seen time-lapse baking videos. If you haven't, I highly recommend checking them out. You'll see speedy versions of boules and baguettes going into the oven and puffing up dramatically before darkening in color and coming back down a bit before being pulled from the heat.

This is "oven spring"—in the first 10 minutes of baking, loaves will increase in size as the yeast activates with the heat, creating gas and bringing your bread to its final shape and volume. Once the crust firms up and yeast begins to die off (around 130°F), the loaf stops expanding and begins to deepen in color. Moisture escapes, giving the bread a light weight for its size, and there you have it: a fantastic loaf of crusty, deeply browned bread.

Developing the perfect crust

Although we home bakers may not have the wood-fired or deck ovens that they have at French boulangeries, there's no reason we can't attempt to re-create that environment. Baking in a preheated Dutch oven (cocotte) or on a preheated baking stone can help. The former can also trap steam created as bread bakes, slowing the formation of the crust and allowing for greater oven spring. The crust will also absorb moisture, which will give it the crackly, light crunch we're used to seeing in really fine loaves. Gelatinized starches on the crust give it shine, and the preheated surface of the cocotte can help get the bottom of the loaf baking as well; the bottom typically needs more time to develop color and crispness than the top.

If you're opposed to preheating your cocotte, or if it's against the manufacturer's recommendations, you can proof the bread right in the Dutch oven and put it into the oven at room temperature. You may lose a bit of the acceleration you get from preheating, but you will still trap the steam. You may need a few minutes of additional bake time, depending on the recipe.

If you can't use a Dutch oven—if you're making baguettes, for instance —you might spritz the loaf with a spray bottle four or five times before it goes in the oven, then repeat a couple of times within the first minutes of the loaf going into the oven, to steam the loaves; this delays crust formation. There are some other ways to do this, too: You can put a cast-iron skillet or cake pan on the bottom rack of your oven before preheating, then once the bread goes in, add about an inch of boiling water or a few ice cubes to the pan. Or, you can brush the loaves generously with water before putting them in the oven, to protect the crust a bit in the same way. Whichever method you choose, you should add steam at the very beginning of baking and once or twice more, after the bread has been baking for 3 minutes, to ensure the steam doesn't all evaporate before doing its job.

Is it done?

If you've fully proofed the dough before baking it, you should end up with a well-browned crust and a light interior. When you're new to baking, taking the internal temperature of the bread with an instant-read thermometer can help you be sure that the bread has baked through. It should be 190°F to 200°F, depending on the type of bread (see each recipe for notes). The bread should also be light for its size and a beautiful deep golden brown. If the bread feels heavy as you lift it out of the oven, don't be afraid to check its internal temperature and put it back in for a few more minutes if it's underdone, decreasing the oven temperature by 25°F or placing the lid back on the Dutch oven if the crust is getting too brown. Cool the loaves on a rack to ensure that the bottom crust does not become soggy. (If the loaf was baked in a Dutch oven, you can use the parchment paper you used to lower the loaf in as a sling to pull it out and transfer it to a cooling rack.) And although it's super tempting to cut into a hot loaf, hold off—the crumb will be best if you let it cool completely before cutting. But no judgment from me if you can't wait; you earned it.

French Bread FAQ and Troubleshooting Guide

How do I know if my yeast is active?
If stored properly, yeast should remain active until its expiration date. But when in doubt, combine the yeast with the liquid in your recipe, and set it aside for 10 minutes. The mixture should look foamy and bubbly once the time is up.

Can I use all-purpose flour?
In the United States, wheat flour is labeled by what it's best used for, and the main types you'll see in a supermarket are bread flour, all-purpose flour (bleached and unbleached—you want unbleached for breads), pastry flour, and cake flour. Bread flours typically contain higher levels of protein, which means they offer more gluten development and a stronger structure in the finished bread. If you swap bread flour for lower-protein all-purpose flour, you may find the loaf lacks strength and won't hold its shape as well. In any

case, don't use cake flour or pastry flour for bread—they are milled much finer and are specifically formulated to have less gluten. All-purpose flour, while imperfect, will still make decent bread. (And don't use self-rising flour for bread, either!)

Does the temperature of the ingredients matter?
Professional bakers sometimes use desired dough temperature formulas to determine the temperature of the liquid being added to their recipe. They do this by measuring the room temperature, flour temperature, and friction factor (temperature increase in dough caused by mixing). Once these numbers are in place, they calculate the temperature of the water or liquid being used in the recipe to achieve a final dough temperature of 75°F to 78°F after kneading. For our purposes, however, we can generalize and say that if you're in a cold environment, it can be helpful to use a slightly warmed liquid to kick-start yeast activity, and if it's a warm day, it can be useful to use a cooler liquid to slow things down so your dough doesn't rise too quickly (which causes a less-stable gluten structure and produces less flavor).

Why should I use a preferment?
A preferment is a portion of a dough made ahead and added to the final mix to improve flavor and texture. You don't need a preferment, but using one can really take your bread to the next level. Letting more gluten develop during initial fermentation makes the dough stronger and gives it a more nuanced flavor. Breads made with preferments are also known to stay fresh for longer periods of time, due to their higher acidity. In this book we'll be using a type of preferment called pâte fermentée in several recipes, including baguettes, boule de pain, pain de campagne, and pain complet.
  If you're short on time and prefer to skip the preferment, you can add the quantities of ingredients used for the preferment into the dough mix and proceed with the recipe as written.

Can I use a baguette pan to keep my baguettes from spreading?
The short answer is yes. You can absolutely use a baguette pan if you'd like to invest in one. Keep in mind that professional bakers typically do not use them; they usually rely on a baker's couche (a linen cloth used during proofing to keep the baguette shape intact). We'll talk about shaping baguettes and proofing them using the tools you have available, but if a

baguette pan helps you feel more comfortable with the process, there's definitely no harm in having one.

How will I know if my bread is ready to bake?
When it comes to the dough's final rise, you're looking for an increase in volume and a marshmallow-y texture. To determine if dough is fully proofed, do a poke test. Here's how: Poke an inconspicuous area of your loaf and watch it spring back. Does it feel firm to the touch and spring back quickly? It needs more time. Does your finger leave an indent that doesn't spring back at all? It may be over-proofed. Does it spring back slowly and leave a bit of an indent behind? Perfect!

  If you've accidentally over-proofed your loaf to the point where it looks like it will immediately deflate if you touch it, go through the shaping process again, set it aside to proof again, and keep a close eye on it! If you think it is barely over-proofed—perhaps it's leaving a deep indent when poked and it looks on the verge of being overinflated—avoid deep scoring, but go ahead and bake per the recipe instructions.

How will my crust brown too quickly?
Have you checked your oven temperature? Typically this happens when an oven is hotter than intended. If you haven't invested in an oven thermometer, you can pick one up for about $5. If your oven runs hot or cold, you'll know it, and you can adjust your temperature accordingly.

How will I know if my loaf is done?
After all the work you put in, you certainly don't want to pull your loaf out and find that it isn't fully baked. These are a few ways to tell if your loaf is ready:

Color: In all the breads in this book, you'll be looking for at least a medium if not deep golden-brown color all over.

Weight: The bread should feel light for its size.

Sound: A fully baked loaf should sound somewhat hollow when you knock on its underside.

Internal temperature: If in doubt, use an instant-read thermometer to check the internal temperature of the bread. Depending on the type of bread, doneness is achieved at typically between 190°F and 200°F.

Why is my bread dense?

When bread is dense, it's typically because the final rise was rushed or too much flour was kneaded in during shaping. Bread that is baked without being fully proofed will remain gummy and dense in the center. A bread baked at too high a temperature may brown quickly before baking all the way through, which may indicate that your oven is not calibrated correctly. (If you haven't checked your oven temperature lately, test it with a stand-alone oven thermometer.)

BAKING AT HIGH ALTITUDES

High-altitude baking can be tricky, and a lot of trial and error is needed to determine exactly the right combination of ingredient quantities, fermentation, and bake time in order to get perfect results. Because there is less air pressure over 3,500 feet, there is less resistance for leavening, which can affect dough production times. Here are some tips to help you get started:

Decrease yeast quantity by 25 percent: Less resistance means a faster rise, which can also mean over-proofing and deflation. Lowering the quantity of yeast can reduce this risk, as can checking the dough during fermentation, because it may need less time to proof.

Cold fermentation: Bulk fermentation in the refrigerator not only adds more flavor, it also makes it easier to control the rise of the dough, because the lower temperature will slow yeast activity.

Using a preferment: Shorter fermentation can mean less flavor, so using a preferment can improve bread's flavor.

Increasing oven temperature: Higher temperatures set crusts quickly, which can help avoid loaves that overexpand, but please note that this might cause a quicker bake time than indicated in the recipes.

ABOUT THE RECIPES

This book offers a variety of classic French loaves. The majority are staple breads, including baguettes, pain de campagne, pain complet, pain aux noix, and brioche. There are also some specialty breads, such as pain brié, le cramique, pain couronne, and fouée, that you might not eat on a daily basis but which are wonderful regional items to learn and to try. Each bread will bring you a unique crust, crumb, and shape, and as you complete each loaf, you'll feel more and more like you've spent time behind the scenes in a boulangerie, exploring the differences in each bread's makeup and discovering your preferences.

I recommend starting with the first recipes, to gain experience with leaner doughs and experiment with preferments before moving on to enriched and laminated doughs. The first hearty loaves in the initial two chapters are foundational, in that they begin to train you not just in mixing and baking techniques but also in developing the intuition that professional bakers rely on so heavily. Kneading will become more enjoyable. You'll begin to notice the scent of the dough and the look of it after bulk fermentation when it's properly risen. When dividing dough, you'll marvel at the way you're able to cut a piece almost exactly to the correct weight in one shot. And when pulling that loaf from the oven, you'll begin to recognize the moment the crust has caramelized to your liking, deep and brown.

Once you move into the sweeter breads and viennoiseries, you'll begin to understand how to develop gluten before fat comes along to inhibit it. You'll appreciate the doughs' supple textures, you'll become more adept at manipulating temperature for easier shaping, and you'll relish the tender interior of the finished products.

All the recipes here include detailed instructions and are designed to show you the simplest method to achieve the best results at home. From here, you can branch out and experiment. You'll find notes about different ways to incorporate your creativity to take each of these loaves up a notch. And as you get more and more familiar with the process of making each item, you'll begin to develop your own tastes when it comes to your perfect loaf.

Every recipe also gives the inactive time, baking time, and time to completion. Please note that this is merely a guide, as the temperature of your kitchen will often determine the length of the process. There are cues in the recipes to show you what to look for in each step. Remember, your life does not have to revolve around the bread. Let the breadmaking process work for you.

Tips

Many of the recipes in this book include tips to help you with your baking.

Baking tip: This is a tip clarifying an instruction or a "keep in mind" note to help make your bake more successful.

Ingredient tip: This is an instruction to help with sourcing, substituting, storing, or using a particular ingredient.

Variation tip: This is a way of tweaking the recipe to get a unique final result.

I hope these small notes will help expand your breadth of knowledge even further and make you feel even more confident throughout your breadmaking journey.

<u>Boule de Pain</u> and <u>Brioche</u>

Baguettes

CHAPTER 2
CRUSTY AND DELICATE

<u>Baguettes</u>
<u>Pain d'Épi</u>
<u>Fougasse</u>
<u>Pain Couronne</u>
<u>Fouée</u>

With these beloved French breads, four ingredients (water, flour, yeast, and salt) come together in lean doughs to create magic. There's no fat, milk, or eggs to give these breads a rich texture or a tender crumb. But when these four ingredients combine—when they're worked together, given time to rest and develop their flavor, and baked well—you end up with the perfect bite. These loaves have thin, crackling crusts, and they have an open crumb made up of feathery wisps of dough.

The breads in this chapter include the classic baguette and the pain d'épi, which is cut to resemble a stalk of wheat. There's also a fougasse, made with a lean dough with a bit of fat added along the way for additional crispness, which is shaped with fun cuts. And we also have a pain couronne, shaped like a crown. Finally, we have fouée, which are rolled to thin rounds like pita, then baked in a hot oven where they puff dramatically to give you perfect pockets for filling.

This chapter is the perfect start on your breadmaking journey. Remember: Knead heartily, have patience, shape gently, and bake deeply. You're on your way.

Baguettes

Here's some good news: You can absolutely make bakery-quality baguettes at home. A combination of spraying the loaves with water and baking at a high temperature ensures good oven spring. The more you practice shaping and scoring your loaves, the more beautiful they will look over time.

Makes: 4 loaves

Prep time: Active: 40 minutes; Inactive: 4 hours 10 minutes

Bake time: 25 minutes

Total time: 5 hours 15 minutes

EQUIPMENT
- Medium bowl or stand mixer with dough hook
- Wooden spoon or dough whisk
- Linen towel or plastic wrap
- Bench scrapers (plastic and metal)
- Kitchen scale (optional)
- Linen towel or couche (proofing cloth)
- Heavy baking sheet
- Baking stone (optional)
- Parchment paper
- Lame or razor
- Spray bottle filled with water
- Cooling rack

1¾ cups (400 grams) water, at room temperature, divided

2 teaspoons (6 grams) instant yeast, divided

5 cups minus 1½ tablespoons (590 grams) bread flour (or T55 flour), divided, plus more for shaping

1 tablespoon (9 grams) kosher salt

1. Make a pâte fermentée: In a medium bowl, stir together ½ cup (100 grams) of water with a pinch of yeast. Add 1¼ cups (150 grams) of flour and 1 teaspoon (3 grams) of salt. Stir until a shaggy dough comes together. Turn the dough onto your bench and knead until well combined, 1 to 2 minutes. The mixture will be sticky. Return the dough to the bowl, cover with a towel, and set aside for 2 to 4 hours at room temperature or refrigerate overnight. It should double in size.

2. Make the dough: Add the remaining 1¼ cups (300 grams) of water and remaining yeast to the pâte fermentée, using your fingers to break up the dough into the liquid. Add the remaining 3⅔ cups (440 grams) of flour and the remaining 2 teaspoons (6 grams) of salt. Mix until a shaggy dough forms, about 1 minute.

3. Turn the dough out onto a clean bench and knead for 8 to 10 minutes (or transfer to a stand mixer and knead for 6 to 8 minutes at low speed) until it is smooth, stretchy, and supple. If you're kneading by hand, resist the urge to add more flour; the dough will naturally become less sticky as you work it.

4. Stretch the dough to check for proper gluten development. If it rips too quickly and feels rough, continue to knead until smooth and supple.

5. If kneading by hand, return the dough to the bowl. Cover with a towel and set aside for 1 hour or until doubled in size. (This timing will vary, depending on your kitchen temperature.)

6. Shape and bake: Lightly flour your bench and use a plastic bench scraper to release the dough from the bowl. Use a metal bench scraper to portion the dough into 4 equal sections (about 250 grams each). Cover with a towel and rest for 5 to 10 minutes.

7. Working with one section at a time, use your fingertips to gently press the dough into a rough rectangle (photo A). Fold the top quarter down to the center (photo B), then fold the bottom quarter up to the center, so they meet. Press lightly along the seam to adhere (photo C).

C

8. Fold the top half of the dough over the bottom half to create a log. Use the heel of your hand or your fingertips to seal the seam (photo D). Make sure your bench is lightly floured. You don't want too much pressure on the dough, but neither do you want it to slide instead of roll. If the dough slides, brush away excess flour and wet your hands lightly.

9. Gently flip the dough so the seam is on the bottom, and use your hands to rock the ends of the loaf back and forth to create a football shape. Then work your hands from the center of the loaf out toward the edges to elongate it to 12 to 14 inches (photo E). Repeat with the remaining sections.

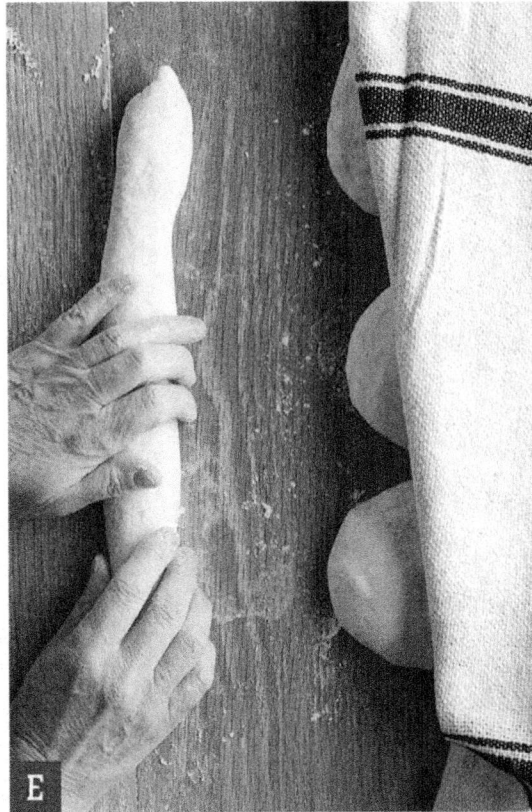

E

10. Lay a linen couche or towel (see Tip) on a baking sheet. Dust it with flour, and fold one end to create a border. Place one baguette next to this fold. Fold the towel along the other side to create a dedicated space for the baguette to rise. Lay another baguette alongside and create another fold. Repeat with the remaining baguettes (photo F).

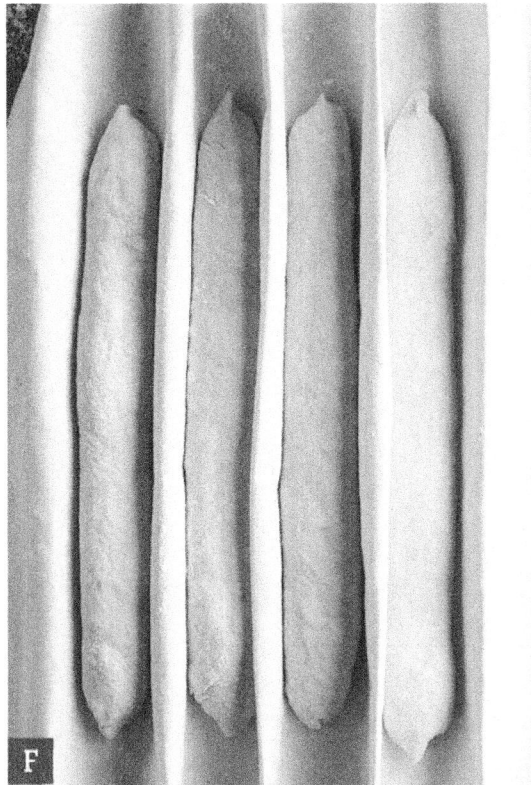

F

11. Cover with a towel and set aside to proof for 1 hour.

12. After 30 minutes of proofing, preheat the oven to 475°F. Set a baking stone (if using) on the center rack. Line a flat baking sheet with parchment paper (flip the baking sheet over and work on the back if using a baking stone).

13. Check the baguettes by poking the dough. It should spring back slightly, leaving an indent, and feel like a marshmallow.

14. When the baguettes are ready to bake, gently lift and transfer them to the prepared baking sheet, placing them 2 inches apart. Take care not to deflate the baguettes while transferring them.

15. Holding a lame or a razor blade at a 30-degree angle, quickly but lightly score five lines diagonally across the top of the baguettes,

about ¼ inch deep and 2 inches apart (photo G). Between loaves, dip the blade into water to release any sticky dough.

16. Put the baking sheet in the oven, or, if using a baking stone, slide the parchment paper from the sheet onto the baking stone. Spritz the loaves with water 4 or 5 times in total and close the oven door. Spray again after 3 minutes of baking, and again after another 3 minutes, working quickly each time to not lose oven heat. Bake for 24 to 28 minutes total, until the loaves are a deep golden brown.

17. Transfer the loaves to a cooling rack for 15 to 20 minutes before cutting.

Baking tip: A couche, or proofing cloth, is used by French bakers to hold free-form breads such as baguettes in their elongated shape while proofing. Traditional couches are made from heavy linen with finished seams; if you can't find one, feel free to substitute a clean linen or cotton dish towel—a smooth weave, not terry cloth. Just make sure it's lint-free, and dust it with flour.

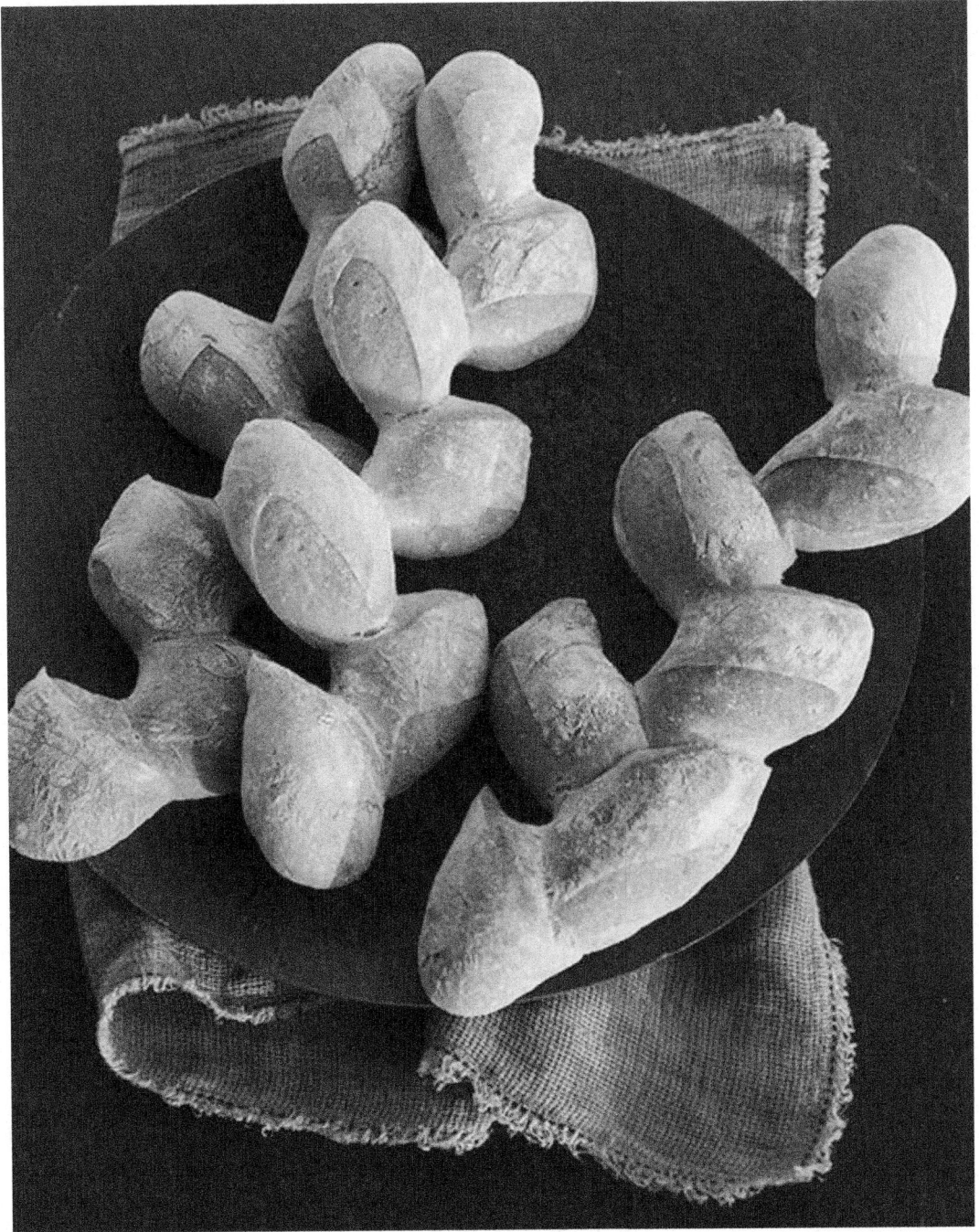

Pain d'Épi

A close relative of the baguette, pain d'épi turns that iconic loaf into something spectacular. The techniques are the same as for classic baguettes, but we cut each loaf to create a "wheat stalk" (épi). The technique is simple, but the result is impressive. Each piece of this bread is designed to be torn off the main loaf, making it a perfect bread for sharing.

Makes: 4 loaves

Prep time: Active: 50 minutes; Inactive: 4 hours 10 minutes

Bake time: 20 minutes

Total time: 5 hours 20 minutes

EQUIPMENT

• Medium bowl or stand mixer with dough hook

• Wooden spoon or dough whisk

• Linen towels or plastic wrap

• Bench scrapers (plastic and metal)

• Kitchen scale (optional)

• 2 heavy baking sheets

• Parchment paper

• Kitchen shears

• Spray bottle filled with water

• Cooling rack

1¾ cups (400 grams) water, at room temperature, divided

2 teaspoons (6 grams) instant yeast, divided

5 cups minus 1½ tablespoons (590 grams) bread flour (or T55 flour), divided, plus more for shaping

1 tablespoon (9 grams) kosher salt

1. Make a pâte fermentée: In a medium bowl, stir together ½ cup (100 grams) of water with a pinch of yeast. Add 1¼ cups (150 grams) of flour and 1 teaspoon (3 grams) of salt. Stir until a shaggy dough comes together. Turn the dough onto your bench and knead until well combined, 1 to 2 minutes. The mixture will be sticky. Return the dough to the bowl, cover with a towel, and set aside for 2 to 4 hours at room temperature or refrigerate overnight. It should double in size.

2. Make the dough: Add the remaining 1¼ cups (300 grams) of water and remaining yeast to the pâte fermentée, using your fingers to break up the dough into the liquid. Add the remaining 3⅔ cups (440 grams) of flour and the remaining 2 teaspoons (6 grams) of salt and mix until a shaggy dough forms, about 1 minute.

3. Turn the dough out onto a clean bench and knead for 8 to 10 minutes (or transfer to a stand mixer and knead for 6 to 8 minutes at low speed) until smooth, stretchy, and supple. If you're kneading by hand, resist the urge to add more flour; the dough will naturally become less sticky as you work it.

4. Stretch the dough to check for proper gluten development. If it rips too quickly and feels rough, continue to knead until smooth and supple.

5. If kneading by hand, return the dough to the bowl. Cover with a towel and set aside for 1 hour or until doubled in size. (This timing will vary, depending on your kitchen temperature.)

6. Shape and bake (see step-by-step images in baguette recipe, for steps 6 through 9): Lightly flour your bench and use a plastic bench scraper to release the dough from the bowl. Use a metal bench scraper to portion the dough into 4 equal sections (about 250 grams each). Cover with a towel and rest for 5 to 10 minutes.

7. Working with one section at a time, use your fingertips to gently press the dough into a rough rectangle. Fold the top quarter down

to the center, then fold the bottom quarter up to the center, so they meet.

8. Press lightly along the seam to adhere. Fold the top half of the dough over the bottom half to create a log. Use the heel of your hand or your fingertips to seal the seam.

9. Gently flip the dough so the seam is on the bottom, and use your hands to rock the ends of the loaf back and forth to create a football shape. Then work your hands from the center of the loaf out toward the edges to elongate it to 12 to 14 inches. Repeat with the remaining sections.

10. Line two baking sheets with parchment paper. Gently transfer two loaves to each prepared baking sheet, spacing them 4 to 5 inches apart.

11. Holding the shears at a 45-degree angle, cut into one baguette about 2 inches from the end (cutting almost all the way through the loaf, in one swipe, so the scissor tips are only about 1/8 inch from the end of the dough) (photo A). Immediately but gently lay the piece to the right side. Make a second cut about 2 inches along the loaf and lay the piece of dough to the left. Repeat, alternating the side to which you're moving the dough, until you've cut the whole loaf (photos B and C). It should resemble a stalk of wheat. Repeat with the remaining loaves.

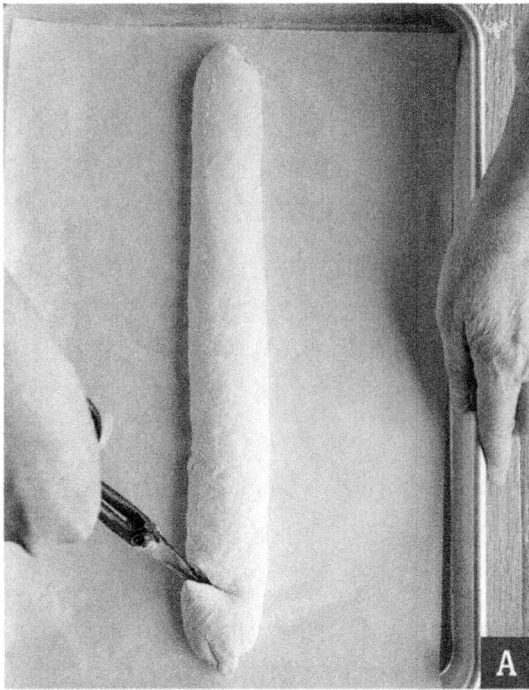

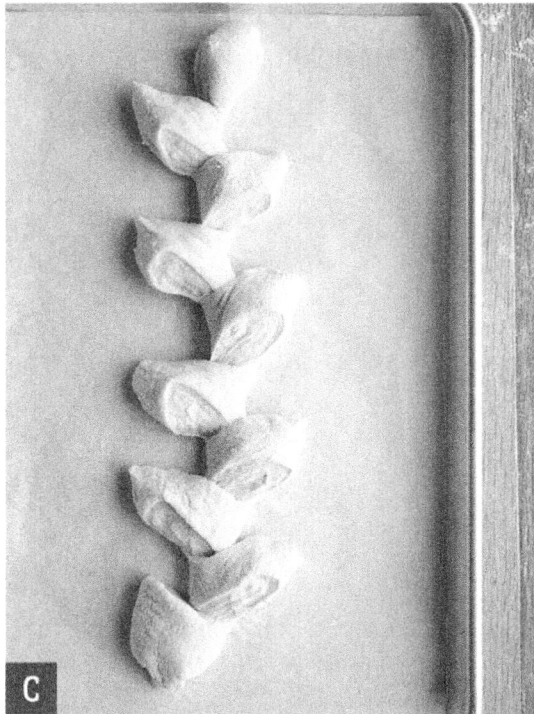

C

12. Cover with towels and set aside to proof for 1 hour or until marshmallow-y in texture. If you poke the dough, it should spring back slightly, leaving an indent. After 30 minutes of proofing, preheat the oven to 475°F.

13. When the loaves are ready to bake, put the baking sheets in the oven. Spritz the loaves with water 4 or 5 times in total and close the door. Spray again after 3 minutes of baking, and again after another 3 minutes, working quickly to not lose oven heat. Bake for 24 to 28 minutes total, rotating the position of the trays halfway through baking for even browning, until the loaves are a deep golden brown.

14. Transfer the loaves to a cooling rack for 10 to 15 minutes before serving.

Variation tip: Get the whole family involved by pre-shaping the baguettes, then having everyone cut their own "wheat stalk." A light brush of egg wash or water can make each loaf the perfect canvas for sprinkling with sesame or poppy seeds, grated cheese, or anything you like.

Fougasse

Decorative and deceptively simple to create, fougasse is a type of bread that was originally thrown into wood fired ovens as a way of assessing their temperature. If the fougasse was baked well, the other breads could be loaded in. These days, fougasse is baked for its own merit. It's a crusty loaf that lends itself to being dotted with herbs, olives, or cheese, or being dipped into olive oil and enjoyed while still warm. And because its shape can be whatever you want it to be, it's also an excellent canvas for getting creative. Simple cuts can create leaflike patterns, rectangular ladders, or even intricate rounds.

Makes: **4 loaves**

Prep time: **Active: 40 minutes; Inactive: 4 hours 20 minutes**

Bake time: **20 minutes**

Total time: **5 hours 20 minutes**

EQUIPMENT

• Medium bowl or stand mixer with dough hook

• Wooden spoon or dough whisk

• Linen towel or plastic wrap

• Bench scrapers (plastic and metal)

• Kitchen scale (optional)

• Rolling pin (optional)

• 2 heavy baking sheets

• Parchment paper

• Paring knife or pizza cutter

• Spray bottle filled with water

1¾ cups (400 grams) water, at room temperature, divided

2 teaspoons (6 grams) instant yeast, divided

5 cups minus 1½ tablespoons (590 grams) bread flour (or T55 flour), divided, plus more for shaping

2 tablespoons (25 grams) olive oil, plus more for drizzling

1 tablespoon (9 grams) kosher salt, plus more for sprinkling

1. Make a pâte fermentée: In a bowl, stir together ½ cup (100 grams) of water with a pinch of yeast. Add 1¼ cups (150 grams) of flour and 1 teaspoon (3 grams) of salt. Stir until a shaggy dough comes together. Turn the dough onto your bench and knead until well combined, 1 to 2 minutes. The mixture will be sticky. Return the dough to the bowl, cover with a towel, and set aside for 2 to 4 hours at room temperature or refrigerate overnight. It should double in size.

2. Make the dough: Add the remaining 1¼ cups (300 grams) of water and remaining yeast to the pâte fermentée, using your fingers to break up the dough into the liquid. Add the remaining 3⅔ cups (440 grams) of flour, the oil, and the remaining 2 teaspoons (6 grams) of salt and mix until a shaggy dough forms, about 1 minute.

3. Turn out the dough onto a clean bench and knead for 8 to 10 minutes (or transfer to a stand mixer and knead for 6 to 8 minutes at low speed) until smooth, stretchy, and supple. If you're kneading by hand, resist the urge to add more flour; the dough will naturally become less sticky as you work it.

4. Stretch the dough to check for proper gluten development. If it rips too quickly and feels rough, continue to knead until smooth and supple.

5. If kneading by hand, return the dough to the bowl. Cover with a towel and set aside for 1 hour or until doubled in size. (This timing will vary, depending on your kitchen temperature.)

6. Shape and bake: Lightly flour your bench and use a plastic bench scraper to release the dough from the bowl. Use a metal bench scraper to portion the dough into 4 equal sections (about 250 grams

each). Cover with a towel and rest for 5 to 10 minutes. Line two baking sheets with parchment paper.

7. Dust the balls with flour and flatten each to a rough oval a little over ¼ inch thick, using first your fingertips (photo A) and then a rolling pin, if desired (photo B).

B

8. Use a paring knife held at a 45-degree angle to cut decorative lines into the dough. Make sure you cut all the way through the dough, and space the cuts at least ½ inch apart (photos C and D).

9. Gently transfer two loaves to each prepared baking sheet, spacing them a few inches apart. Stretch them gently to make sure the cuts remain open while baking (the holes will shrink and narrow as the bread expands in the oven).

10. Cover the loaves with towels and set aside to proof for 30 to 45 minutes or until marshmallow-y in texture. If you poke the dough, it should spring back slightly, leaving an indent. After 15 minutes of proofing, preheat the oven to 475°F.

11. When the loaves are ready to bake, put the baking sheets in the oven. Spritz the loaves with water 4 or 5 times, and close the door. Spray again after 3 minutes of baking, and again after another 3 minutes, working quickly to not lose oven heat. Bake for 18 to 20 minutes total, until the loaves are a deep golden brown, rotating the position of the trays halfway through baking for even browning. Remove the trays from the oven and set aside to cool slightly.

12. Drizzle with olive oil and sprinkle with salt before serving.

Baking tip: When making decorative cuts in fougasse, think of cutting snowflakes out of paper—no two need to be alike, and you can get creative. It's best to start with fewer, more dramatic cuts as smaller, more delicate cuts will disappear as the dough rises in the oven.

Variation tip: Fougasse is great with the addition of olives, cheese, herbs, or any other flavoring you like. Just knead the dough as directed, then, before setting it aside for bulk fermentation, add about 1 cup of your chosen ingredient and knead it in for 30 seconds to incorporate.

Pain Couronne

Hailing from the Bordeaux region, this ring-shaped loaf looks a bit like a crown (couronne in French). Perfect for holiday gatherings, this festive ring can be made with any type of dough, including pain de campagne. Although it may look difficult to form and score, it is actually assembled with just a few simple steps. If you fall in love with making this bread, a special ring-shaped couronne banneton helps the process go even more quickly. But when you're starting out, the simple workaround in this recipe —using a cake pan and a small bowl, or even a measuring cup—works great.

Makes: 1 ring

Prep time: Active: 50 minutes; Inactive: 2 hours 10 minutes

Bake time: 20 minutes

Total time: 3 hours 20 minutes

EQUIPMENT
- Medium bowl or stand mixer with dough hook
- Wooden spoon or dough whisk
- Linen towels
- Bench scrapers (plastic and metal)
- 3-inch bowl
- 9-inch cake pan
- Rolling pin
- Pastry brush
- Paring knife
- Heavy baking sheet
- Parchment paper
- Spray bottle filled with water
- Cooling rack

1 cup plus 2 tablespoons (255 grams) water, at room temperature

1½ tablespoons (32 grams) honey

1½ teaspoons (4 grams) instant yeast

2 cups (225 grams) whole wheat flour (or T150 flour)

1 cup plus 1 tablespoon (131 grams) bread flour (or T55 flour), plus more for shaping

2 teaspoons (6 grams) kosher salt

1. Make the dough: In a medium bowl, stir together the water, honey, and yeast. Add the whole wheat and bread flours and the salt and stir until a shaggy dough comes together. Turn the dough out onto a clean bench and knead for 8 to 10 minutes (or transfer to a stand mixer and knead for 6 to 8 minutes at low speed) until smooth, stretchy, and supple.

2. Stretch the dough to ensure proper gluten development. If it rips too quickly and feels rough, continue to knead until smooth and supple.

3. If you're kneading by hand, return the dough to the bowl. Cover with a towel and set aside for 1 hour or until doubled in size. (This timing will vary, depending on your kitchen temperature.)

4. Shape and bake: Lightly flour your bench and use a plastic bench scraper to release the dough from the bowl. Use a metal bench scraper to portion the dough into 8 equal pieces (about 80 grams each).

5. Using your fingertips, pull the edges of one piece of dough inward, working around the dough clockwise until all edges are folded into the center (see step-by-step photos in the boule de pain recipe, for method). Pinch lightly to adhere. You should see the folds of dough meeting in the center, creating a seam. Flip each ball over. (Take care to not knead the dough or deflate it too aggressively.) Cup both hands around the base, and using the grip of the table, pull the ball toward you, rotating as you go, to tighten the seam. Repeat with the

remaining balls (photo A). Cover with a towel and rest for 5 to 10 minutes.

A

6. Place the 3-inch bowl upside down in the center of the 9-inch cake pan to form a ring, line it with a towel, and press it down to set the shape (photo B). Dust the towel generously with flour.

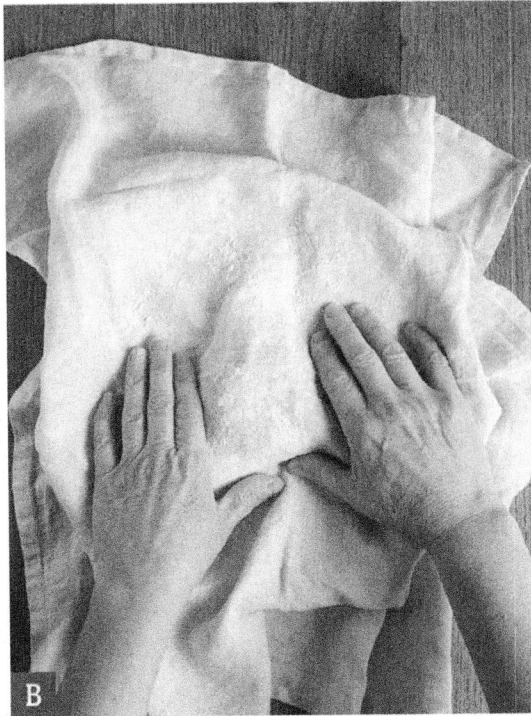

7. Use a rolling pin to roll one dough ball into a ¼-inch-thick, 8-inch-diameter round. If you find the dough is shrinking back, give it more time to rest. Lay this over the bump in the center of the form (photo C). Arrange the remaining dough balls seam-side up around the central piece to create a ring. The balls should cover about ½ inch of the rim of the central piece. Use a pastry brush to dust off excess flour.

8. Take a paring knife and cut a line across the central piece, starting between two balls and finishing between two balls on the opposite side, cutting all the way through (photo D). Repeat until there is a triangle of dough corresponding to each dough ball. (The final cut will only be to the center.)

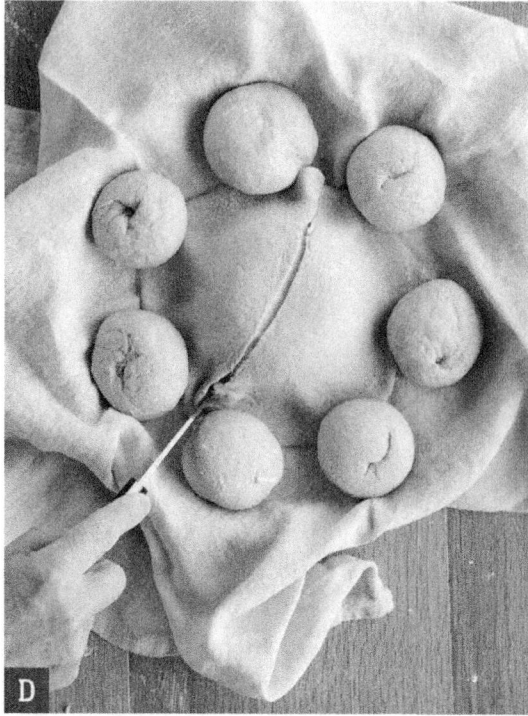

9. Fold the triangles back and drape each one over the corresponding dough ball, pressing lightly to adhere (photo E). Cover with a towel and set aside to proof for about 1 hour until marshmallow-y in texture. If you poke the dough, it should spring back slightly, leaving an indent.

10. After 30 minutes of proofing, preheat the oven to 450°F. Line a baking sheet with parchment paper.

11. When the loaf is ready to bake, gently flip the form onto the prepared baking sheet (photo F). Pull away the form and towel to reveal a crown shape. Put the baking sheet in the oven. Spritz the loaf with water 4 or 5 times, and close the door. Spray again after 3 minutes of baking, and again after another 3 minutes, working quickly to not lose oven heat. Bake for 20 to 25 minutes total until the loaf is a deep golden brown.

12. Transfer the loaf to a cooling rack for 10 to 15 minutes before serving.

Fouée

If you're a fan of pita bread, fouée will be right up your alley. This airy bread round from western France is typically baked quickly in a wood-fired oven, split open to reveal its hollow center, and filled with pork rillettes and white beans. This recipe must be followed to the letter, because if you roll your dough too thick or deprive it of its final proof it won't puff. Roll it too thin and you'll have a cracker.

Makes: 8 bread rounds

Prep time: **Active: 40 minutes; Inactive: 1 hour 25 minutes**

Bake time: 10 minutes

Total time: 2 hours 15 minutes

EQUIPMENT
- Medium bowl or stand mixer with dough hook
- Wooden spoon or dough whisk
- Linen towel or plastic wrap, for covering
- Bench scrapers (plastic and metal)
- Baking stone or heavy baking sheet
- Rolling pin
- Cooling rack

1½ cups (350 grams) water, at room temperature

2 teaspoons (6 grams) instant yeast

5 cups minus 1½ tablespoons (590 grams) all-purpose flour (or T55 flour), plus more for shaping

1 tablespoon (9 grams) kosher salt

Oil, for greasing baking sheet (optional)

1. Make the dough: In a bowl, combine the water and yeast, then stir in the flour and salt. Knead by hand for 6 to 8 minutes (or 4 to 6 minutes in a stand mixer at low speed) until well combined and smooth. If working in a mixer, you may need to finish the dough by hand, as it's a bit heavy. Cover with a towel or plastic wrap, and set aside for 1 hour or until doubled in size. This will vary depending on your kitchen temperature.

2. Shape and bake: Lightly flour your bench and use a plastic bench scraper to release the dough from the bowl. Use a metal bench scraper to portion into 8 equal pieces, about 115 grams each.

3. Using your fingertips, pull the edges of one piece of dough inward, working around the dough clockwise until all edges are folded into the center (see step-by-step photos in the boule de pain recipe, for method). Pinch lightly to adhere. You should see the folds of dough meeting in the center, creating a seam. (Take care to not knead the dough or deflate it too aggressively.)

4. Flip each round over. Cup both hands around the base, and using the grip of the table, pull the round toward you, rotating as you go, to tighten the seam. Repeat with the remaining rounds. Cover with a towel and rest for 5 to 10 minutes.

5. Transfer 4 rounds to a small plate, cover with a towel or plastic wrap, and transfer to the refrigerator. Cover the remaining rounds and rest for 5 to 10 minutes.

6. Preheat the oven to 475°F. Put a baking stone or oiled heavy baking sheet on the center rack of the oven.

7. Dust your bench with flour and roll the 4 unrefrigerated dough rounds to ¼-inch-thick circles. Be precise about the thickness: Dough that is too thick will not puff, and those that are too thin will become crackers. If the dough is shrinking back while you're rolling, cover it, rest for an additional 10 minutes, then try again.

8. Proof, uncovered, for 15 to 20 minutes or until lightly puffed. In the meantime, roll out the 4 refrigerated rounds.

9. Quickly and gently place the first 4 pieces on the baking stone or baking sheet, spacing them at least 2 inches apart. Bake for 8 to 10 minutes, until puffed and lightly golden brown in spots.

10. Remove from the oven, set on a cooling rack, and bake the remaining pieces when they're lightly puffed and have rested for 15 to 20 minutes.

11. Cool for 5 to 10 minutes before splitting and filling.

Baking tip: Working with half of the dough at a time will help you get the timing right to avoid some rounds over-proofing while waiting for oven space. If you aren't sure if you're rolling the dough to the correct thickness, refrigerate all the pieces except for one. Test the process with this first round to get the feel for things before you proceed with the whole batch. Keep in mind, the cooler the temperature of the dough, the more time it may need to proof.

Boule de Pain

CHAPTER 3

ROUND AND CHEWY

Boule de Pain
Pain de Campagne
(Sourdough Starter)
Pain Complet
Pain aux Noix
Pain Brié

You've worked with flour, water, salt, and yeast but now we're going to experiment with even more flavor and additional shaping techniques. In this chapter we're focusing on boules (balls) and bâtards (footballs). With the addition of whole wheat and rye flours, we end up with a slightly heavier crumb.

We'll start with boule de pain, using a poolish as our preferment. We'll shape this loaf with a banneton or bowl to keep the structure of the loaf intact during proofing. We'll use a similar technique for pain de campagne, which is made with a levain, a natural sourdough starter. Next comes a pain complet, a whole wheat loaf, which we shape into a bâtard. We use this same shape for pain aux noix, which is made with a bit of whole wheat flour and honey, for enriched flavor, and dotted with walnuts. Then, for something completely different, we'll make pain brié, which uses a pâte fermentée but adds butter. This gives pain brié a tenderness that you don't expect when slicing into it.

Boule de Pain

A boule (ball) is a traditional shape for French bread, and making one is one of the easiest shaping methods to learn. A boule de pain can be made with any type of flour or any mix of dough. Here, I use a bit of whole wheat for more flavor, but feel free to use this shape and baking method for any type of bread you like. Fun fact: Boule is the root of the word boulangers (bread bakers) and boulangeries (bread bakeries)!

Makes: 1 loaf
Prep time: Active: 40 minutes; Inactive: 4 hours
Bake time: 35 minutes
Total time: 5 hours 15 minutes

EQUIPMENT
- Medium bowl or stand mixer with dough hook
- Wooden spoon or dough whisk
- Linen towels or plastic wrap
- Banneton proofing basket or medium bowl lined with linen towel
- Plastic bench scraper
- Baking stone, heavy baking sheet, or Dutch oven with lid
- Lame or razor
- Parchment paper
- Spray bottle filled with water
- Thermometer (optional)

1½ cups (350 grams) water, at room temperature, divided
2 teaspoons (6 grams) instant yeast, divided
3¾ cups (450 grams) bread flour (or T55 flour), divided, plus more for shaping
¼ cup (50 grams) whole wheat flour (or T150 flour)
1 tablespoon (9 grams) kosher salt

1. Make a poolish: In a bowl, stir together ¾ cup plus 2 tablespoons (200 grams) of water with a pinch of yeast. Add 1¾ cups (200 grams) of bread flour. Stir until a smooth paste forms. Cover with a towel and set aside for 2 to 4 hours at room temperature or refrigerate overnight. It should double in size.

2. Make the dough: Add the remaining ⅔ cup (150 grams) of water and remaining yeast to the poolish, using your fingers to break up the dough into the liquid. Add the remaining 2 cups (250 grams) of bread flour, the whole wheat flour, and the salt, and mix until a shaggy dough forms, about 1 minute. Turn the dough out onto a clean bench and knead for 8 to 10 minutes (or transfer to a stand mixer and knead for 6 to 8 minutes at low speed) until the dough is smooth, stretchy, and supple. If you're kneading by hand, resist the urge to add more flour; the dough will naturally become less sticky as you work it.

3. Stretch the dough to check for proper gluten development. If it rips too quickly and feels rough, continue to knead until smooth and supple.

4. If kneading by hand, return the dough to the bowl. Cover with a towel and set aside for 1 hour or until doubled in size. (This timing will vary, depending on your kitchen temperature.)

5. Shape and bake: Flour a banneton shaping basket or a bowl lined with a towel. Lightly flour your bench and use a plastic bench scraper to release the dough from the bowl.

6. Using your fingertips, pull the edges of the dough inward (photo A), working around the dough clockwise until all edges are folded into the center. Pinch lightly to adhere (photo B). You should see the folds of dough meeting in the center, creating a seam. (Take care to not knead the dough or deflate it too aggressively.)

B

7. Flip the dough over. Cup both hands around the base, and using the grip of the table, pull the round toward you, rotating as you go, to tighten the seam. Flour the smooth top and place the round, seam-side up, in the prepared basket or bowl.

8. Cover with a towel and set aside to proof for 1 to 1½ hours, until light in texture and doubled in volume. If you poke the dough, it should spring back slightly, leaving an indent. After 30 minutes of proofing, preheat the oven to 475°F with a baking stone, baking sheet, or Dutch oven (with its lid) inside to heat up as the oven heats.

9. When the loaf is ready to bake, gently flip it onto a 10- to 12-inch square of parchment paper. Use a lame or razor to decoratively score, using quick, light movements (photos C and D; see Tip).

D

10. Slide the proofed loaf on the parchment paper onto a baking sheet and put in the preheated oven. If using a baking stone, slide the parchment paper with the loaf on it onto the back of a baking sheet, then from the baking sheet onto the heated baking stone in the oven. (If using a Dutch oven, skip to step 12.)

11. Reduce the oven temperature to 450°F, spritz the loaf with water 4 or 5 times, and close the door. Spray again after 3 minutes of baking, and again after another 3 minutes, working quickly each time to not lose oven heat. Bake for 25 to 30 minutes total until the crust is a deep golden brown and a temperature probe inserted into the center of the loaf registers about 200°F. (I like to check the temperature by inserting the probe into the side of the loaf, rather than the top, so the hole is discreet.) Slide the loaf onto a cooling rack.

12. If you're using a Dutch oven, remove the pot from the oven, uncover it, and lower the loaf inside using the parchment paper. Cover and bake for 20 minutes, then remove the lid and bake for an additional 10 to 15 minutes until the loaf is a deep golden brown and the temperature registers about 200°F. Use the edges of the parchment paper like a sling to lift the loaf out of the pot and onto a cooling rack. (It is unnecessary to spritz loaves made in a Dutch oven or cocotte, as the closed pot allows the loaf to steam itself.)

13. Let the loaf cool for 15 to 20 minutes before slicing.

Baking tip: Scoring is decorative and serves a purpose—it helps the bread expand in the oven. Scoring a boule can be as simple as making a slash down the center, or as detailed as making an etching of autumn leaves. This is your chance to carve your baker's signature into your work—enjoy the process! A traditional and simple scoring technique for boules is to angle the lame at 30 degrees and score one curved ¼-inch-deep line down the center of the loaf, pulling toward you. Another is a windowpane design, angling your lame at 90 degrees and drawing two parallel lines, and then cutting two parallel lines in the alternate direction to create a crosshatch about ¼ inch deep (see the photos here). If you don't feel confident about making cuts, use a stencil to sift a little flour onto the loaf in a beautiful design before baking it.

Pain de Campagne

Pain de campagne, a sourdough bread, is typically baked as a large round (miche), though you can also give it a more oblong shape. It gets its earthy flavor and moist texture from rye flour and a sourdough starter. Villages in France used to have communal ovens where everyone would bake these, and the loaves could weigh up to 12 pounds! I've included instructions for making a sourdough starter.

Makes: 1 loaf

Prep time: **Active: 35 minutes; Inactive: 2 hours**

Bake time: **35 minutes**

Total time: 3 hours 10 minutes

EQUIPMENT

- Medium bowl or stand mixer with dough hook
- Wooden spoon or dough whisk
- Linen towel or plastic wrap
- Banneton shaping basket or medium bowl lined with linen towel
- Plastic bench scraper
- Baking stone, heavy baking sheet, or Dutch oven
- Parchment paper
- Lame or razor
- Spray bottle filled with water
- Thermometer (optional)
- Cooling rack

¼ cup (60 grams) Sourdough Starter or pâte fermentée (here)

1¼ cups (290 grams) water, at room temperature

2¾ cups plus 1 tablespoon (340 grams) bread flour (or T55 flour), plus more for shaping

⅔ cup (75 grams) rye flour (or T170 flour)
1 tablespoon (9 grams) kosher salt

1. Make the dough: In a medium bowl, stir together the sourdough starter, water, bread flour, and rye flour. Add the salt and stir until a shaggy dough comes together. Turn the dough onto a clean bench and knead for 8 to 10 minutes (or transfer to a stand mixer and knead for 6 to 8 minutes at low speed) until smooth, stretchy, and supple. If you're kneading by hand, resist the urge to add more flour; the dough will naturally become less sticky as you work it.

2. Stretch the dough to check for proper gluten development. If it rips too quickly and feels rough in texture, continue to knead until smooth and supple texture.

3. If kneading by hand, return the dough to the bowl. Cover with a towel and set aside for 1 to 3 hours or until doubled in size. (This timing will vary depending on your kitchen temperature and the starter's activity level.)

4. Shape and bake (see step-by-step photos in the boule de pain recipe, for method): Flour a banneton or bowl lined with a towel. Lightly flour your bench and use a plastic bench scraper to release the dough from the bowl.

5. Using your fingertips, pull the edges of the dough inward, working around the dough clockwise until all edges are folded into the center. Pinch lightly to adhere. You should see the folds of dough meeting in the center, creating a seam. (Take care to not knead the dough or deflate it too aggressively.) Flip the dough over. Flour the smooth top of the dough, and place the round, seam-side up, in the prepared basket. For a loaf with a ringed pattern, remove the liner from the proofing basket and flour before placing the dough inside.

6. Cover with a towel and set aside to proof for 1 to 1½ hours until light in texture and doubled in volume. If you poke the dough, it should spring back slightly, leaving an indent. After 30 minutes of

proofing, preheat the oven to 475°F with a baking stone, baking sheet, or Dutch oven (with its lid) inside to heat up as the oven heats.

7. When the loaf is ready to bake, gently flip it onto a 10- to 12-inch square of parchment paper. Hold a lame at 90 degrees and using quick, light movements, score a large X in the center of the loaf, ¼ inch deep.

8. If using a baking sheet, flip the proofed loaf onto a baking sheet lined with parchment paper and place in the preheated oven. If using a baking stone, slide the parchment paper with the loaf on it onto the back of a baking sheet, then from the baking sheet onto the heated baking stone in the oven. (If using a Dutch oven, skip to step 10.)

9. Reduce the oven temperature to 450°F, spritz the loaf with water 4 or 5 times, and close the door. Spray again after 3 minutes of baking, then again after another 3 minutes, working quickly each time to not lose oven heat. Bake for 25 to 30 minutes total, until the crust is a deep golden brown and a temperature probe inserted into the center of the loaf registers about 205°F. Use the parchment paper to slide the loaf out of the oven and onto a cooling rack.

10. If using a Dutch oven or cocotte: Remove the pot from the oven, uncover it, and lower the loaf in using the parchment paper. Cover and bake for 20 minutes, then remove the lid and bake for an additional 10 to 15 minutes until the loaf is a deep golden brown. Use the edges of the parchment paper like a sling to lift the loaf out of the pot and onto a cooling rack. (It is unnecessary to spritz loaves made in a Dutch oven or cocotte, as the closed pot allows the loaf to steam itself.)

11. Let the loaf sit for 15 to 20 minutes before slicing.

Variation tip: No time to make a sourdough starter? Use a pâte fermentée instead. In a medium bowl, stir together ½ cup (120 grams) water with ¼ teaspoon instant yeast. Add ¾ cup (90 grams) bread flour and ⅓ cup (37 grams) rye flour, and stir to a paste. Cover and set aside for 2 to 4 hours at room temperature or refrigerate overnight. It should double in size. Add another ¾ cup (170 grams) water and another 1 ¾ teaspoons instant yeast, using your fingers to break up the dough into the liquid. It should feel stringy. Add another 2 cups plus 1 tablespoon (250 grams) bread flour, ⅓ cup (37 grams) rye flour, and 1 tablespoon of salt and mix until a shaggy dough forms, 1 to 2 minutes. Continue with the recipe from this point in step 1.

Sourdough Starter

Follow this recipe and schedule for a starter that can be used after seven days (although it will still be young in terms of flavor development).

½ cup (56 grams) rye flour

2¾ cups (616 grams) water, at room emperature, divided

5 cups (600 grams) all-purpose flour, divided

Day 1: In a glass, plastic, or stainless steel container, stir together ½ cup (56 grams) rye flour with ¼ cup (56 grams) water. Cover loosely and set aside for 24 hours, ideally at 68°F to 72°F.

Days 2 and 3: Weigh or measure the total amount of starter and discard half. Add ½ cup (60 grams) all-purpose flour and ¼ cup (56 grams) water and stir to combine. Cover loosely and set aside for 24 hours.

Days 4 to 6: Repeat the instructions for days 2 and 3, but set aside for 12 hours between feedings (in other words, feed twice per day).

Day 7: Measure out ½ cup (113 grams) of starter and discard the rest. Add ½ cup (60 grams) all-purpose flour and ¼ cup (56 grams) water and stir to combine. Cover loosely and set aside for 4 to 6 hours. You can now measure out the ¼ cup (60 grams) needed for pain de campagne. Store the remaining starter in the refrigerator, loosely covered, and feed it 1 to 2 times per week. Before using, remove from the refrigerator and repeat day 4 for 2 days to activate the starter.

Pain Complet

Pain complet is a whole wheat loaf in its purest form. Slightly dense in texture, it's wonderful for sandwiches or enjoyed at breakfast with a spoonful of jam, pat of butter, drizzle of honey, or dollop of marmalade. Here, we've shaped it into a bâtard. You can play with the proportions of flour to work with other whole grain blends or incorporate some bread flour for a slightly more open crumb.

Makes: 1 loaf

Prep time: **Active: 30 minutes; Inactive: 4 hours 10 minutes**

Bake time: 25 minutes

Total time: **5 hours 5 minutes**

EQUIPMENT
- Medium bowl or stand mixer with dough hook
- Wooden spoon or dough whisk
- Linen towel or plastic wrap
- Plastic bench scraper
- Heavy baking sheet
- Parchment paper
- Lame or razor
- Spray bottle filled with water
- Thermometer (optional)
- Cooling rack

¾ cup (175 grams) water, at room temperature, divided

2 tablespoons (42 grams) honey

1½ teaspoons (4 grams) instant yeast, divided

2¼ cups (250 grams) whole wheat flour (or T150 flour), divided, plus more for shaping

1½ teaspoons (5 grams) kosher salt

1. Make a poolish: In a medium bowl, stir together ½ cup (100 grams) of water, the honey, and a pinch of yeast, then a scant 1 cup (100 grams) of flour. Stir until a thick paste forms. Cover with a towel and set aside for 2 to 4 hours at room temperature or refrigerate overnight. It should double in size.

2. Make the dough: Add the remaining ¼ cup (75 grams) of water and remaining yeast to the preferment, using your fingers to break up the dough into the liquid. Add the remaining 1¼ cups (150 grams) of flour and the salt, and mix until a shaggy dough forms, about 1 minute. Turn the dough out onto a clean bench and knead for 8 to 10 minutes (or transfer to a stand mixer and knead for 6 to 8 minutes at low speed) until smooth, stretchy, and supple. If you're kneading by hand, resist the urge to add more flour; the dough will naturally become less sticky as you work it. If kneading by hand, return the dough to the bowl. Cover with a towel and set it aside for 1 hour or until doubled in size. (This timing will vary, depending on your kitchen temperature.)

3. Shape and bake: Lightly flour your bench and use a plastic bench scraper to release the dough from the bowl.

4. Using your fingertips, pull the edges of the dough inward, working around the dough clockwise until all edges are folded into the center. Pinch lightly to adhere (see step-by-step photos in the boule de pain recipe, for method). You should see the folds of dough meeting in the center, creating a seam. (Take care to not knead the dough or deflate it too aggressively.) Flip the dough over. Cup both hands around the base and, using the grip of the table, pull the round toward you, rotating as you go, to tighten the seam. Cover with a towel and rest for 5 to 10 minutes.

5. Use your fingertips to gently press the round to a rough oval (photo A). Fold the top third of the dough toward you and press

lightly along the seam to adhere. Roll the dough over itself toward you again, to create a log (photo B), using the heel of your hand or your fingertips to seal the seam. Make sure your bench is lightly floured. You don't want too much pressure on the dough, but nor do you want the dough to slide instead of roll. If the dough slides, brush away excess flour and wet your hands lightly.

6. Gently flip the dough so the seam is on the bottom, and use your hands to rock the ends of the loaf back and forth to create a football shape (bâtard). Then work your hands from the center of the loaf out toward the edges to elongate it slightly to about 8 inches long (photo C). Transfer to a baking sheet lined with parchment paper.

7. Cover the dough with a towel and set aside for about 1 hour, until it has a marshmallow-y texture. If you poke the dough, it should spring back slightly, leaving an indent. After 30 minutes of proofing, preheat the oven to 450°F.

8. When the loaf is ready to bake, hold a lame at a 30-degree angle and decoratively score, using quick, light movements to create parallel diagonal lines down the length of the loaf. It will look almost like a scored sausage (saucisson) about to be cooked!

9. Put the baking sheet in the oven, spritz the loaf with water 4 or 5 times, and close the door. Spray again after 3 minutes of baking, and again after another 3 minutes, working quickly to not lose oven heat. Bake for 20 to 25 minutes total, until the loaf is a deep golden brown and the internal temperature registers about 200°F.

10. Transfer the loaf to a cooling rack for 15 to 20 minutes before slicing.

Variation tip: If desired, you can coat your loaf with oats or seeds before baking; just brush the exterior of the loaf with egg white or water and sprinkle with your desired topping for a final flourish.

Pain aux Noix

Pain aux noix is a wonderful loaf, and its dough is beautiful to work with. It is made with whole wheat flour, honey, and chopped walnuts (noix), which create a warm and hearty flavor. This bread is perfect for pairing with cheese or foie gras and is great for picnics and sandwiches.

Makes: 2 loaves

Prep time: Active: 30 minutes; Inactive: 2 hours 10 minutes

Bake time: 25 minutes

Total time: 3 hours 5 minutes

EQUIPMENT
- Medium bowl or stand mixer with dough hook
- Wooden spoon or dough whisk
- Linen towel or plastic wrap
- Plastic bench scraper
- Kitchen scale (optional)
- Heavy baking sheet
- Parchment paper
- Lame or razor
- Spray bottle filled with water
- Thermometer (optional)
- Cooling rack

1½ cups (340 grams) water, at room temperature

3 tablespoons (63 grams) honey

2 teaspoons (6 grams) instant yeast

2⅔ cups (300 grams) whole wheat flour (or T150 flour)

Scant 1½ cups (175 grams) bread flour (or T55 flour), plus more for shaping

1 tablespoon (9 grams) kosher salt

1½ cups (135 grams) roughly chopped walnuts

1. Make the dough: In a medium bowl, stir together the water, honey, and yeast. Add the whole wheat and bread flours and salt. Stir until a shaggy dough comes together. Turn the dough onto a clean bench and knead for 8 to 10 minutes (or transfer to a stand mixer and knead for 6 to 8 minutes at low speed) until smooth, stretchy, and supple. Stretch the dough to check for proper gluten development. If it rips too quickly and feels rough, continue to knead until smooth and supple. Knead in the walnuts.

2. If kneading by hand, return the dough to the bowl. Cover with a towel and set aside for 1 hour or until doubled in size. (This timing will vary, depending on your kitchen temperature.)

3. Shape and bake (see step-by-step photos in the pain complet recipe, for method): Lightly flour your bench and use a plastic bench scraper to release the dough from the bowl. Divide the dough in two, using a scale to ensure equal weights, if you have one.

4. Using your fingertips, pull the edges of one piece of dough inward, working around the dough clockwise until all edges are folded into the center. Pinch lightly to adhere. You should see the folds of dough meeting in the center, creating a seam. (Take care to not knead the dough or deflate it too aggressively.) Flip the round over. Cup both hands around the base and, using the grip of the table, pull the round toward you, rotating as you go, to tighten the seam. Repeat with the remaining round. Cover with a towel and rest for 5 to 10 minutes.

5. Working with one round at a time, gently press it to a rough oval. Fold the top third of the dough toward you and press lightly along the seam to adhere. Roll the dough over itself toward you again to create a log, using the heel of your hand or your fingertips to seal the seam. Make sure your bench is lightly floured. You don't want too much pressure on the dough, but neither do you want it to slide

instead of roll. If the dough slides, brush away excess flour and wet your hands lightly.

6. Gently flip the dough so the seam is on the bottom, and use your hands to rock the ends of the loaf back and forth to create a football shape (bâtard). Then work your hands from the center of each loaf out toward the edges to elongate them slightly, until they're 8 to 10 inches long. Transfer both loaves to a baking sheet lined with parchment paper, spacing them at least a few inches apart.

7. Cover with a towel and set aside to proof for about 1 hour or until marshmallow-y in texture. If you poke the dough, it should spring back slightly, leaving an indent. After 30 minutes of proofing, preheat the oven to 450°F.

8. When the loaves are ready to bake, hold a lame at a 30-degree angle and decoratively score, using quick, light movements to create 2 or 3 parallel diagonal lines down the length of the loaf.

9. Put the baking sheet in the oven, spritz with water 4 or 5 times, and close the door. Spray again after 3 minutes of baking, and again after another 3 minutes, working quickly to not lose oven heat. Bake for 20 to 25 minutes total, until the loaves are a deep golden brown and the internal temperature registers about 190°F.

10. Transfer the loaves to a cooling rack for 15 to 20 minutes before cutting.

Variation tip: The walnuts in this loaf are perfect paired with raisins. If you'd like to add some, soak about 1 cup (145 grams) in warm water overnight, then drain, dry on a paper towel, and add while kneading in the walnuts. Proceed with the recipe as written.

Pain Brié

Pain brié is a traditional bread from Normandy with quite the deceptive name (and look). Its name derives from the word brier (to pound), as it was said that the dough was kneaded and pounded to produce a heavy loaf with a tight crumb. Its somewhat armored look does give the impression of a heavy, dense loaf, but you'll find that the butter incorporated into the preferment of pain brié gives its tight crumb an unexpected tenderness.

Makes: 1 loaf
Prep time: **Active: 30 minutes; Inactive: 4 hours 10 minutes**
Bake time: **25 minutes**
Total time: 5 hours 5 minutes

EQUIPMENT
- Medium bowl or stand mixer with dough hook
- Wooden spoon or dough whisk
- Linen towel or plastic wrap
- Plastic bench scraper
- Heavy baking sheet
- Parchment paper
- Lame or razor
- Spray bottle filled with water
- Thermometer (optional)
- Cooling rack

1 cup plus 2 tablespoons (265 grams) water, at room temperature, divided

2 teaspoons (6 grams) instant yeast, divided

4 cups plus 2 tablespoons (500 grams) all-purpose flour (or T55 flour), divided, plus more for shaping

1 tablespoon (9 grams) kosher salt, divided
Scant 3 tablespoons (40 grams) unsalted butter, at room temperature

1. Make a pâte fermentée: In a medium bowl, stir together ½ cup (120 grams) of water with a pinch of yeast. Add 1⅔ cups (200 grams) of flour and 1 teaspoon (3 grams) of salt. Stir until a shaggy dough comes together. Turn the dough onto your bench and knead until well combined, 1 to 2 minutes. Return the dough to the bowl, cover with a towel, and set aside for 2 to 4 hours at room temperature or refrigerate overnight. It should double in size.

2. Make the dough: Add the remaining ½ cup plus 2 tablespoons (145 grams) of water and remaining yeast to the preferment, using your fingers to break up the dough into the liquid. Lumps are okay. Add the remaining 2⅔ cups plus 2 tablespoons (300 grams) of flour, 2 teaspoons (6 grams) of salt, and the butter. Mix for 1 to 2 minutes, until a shaggy dough forms.

3. Turn the dough onto a clean bench and knead for 8 to 10 minutes (or transfer to a stand mixer and knead for 6 to 8 minutes at low speed) until smooth. (You may need to finish the dough by hand, even if you're using the mixer, due to the dough's density and strength.) If kneading by hand, return the dough to the bowl. Cover with a towel and set aside for 1 hour or until doubled in size. (This timing will vary, depending on your kitchen temperature.)

4. Shape and bake (see step-by-step photos in the pain complet recipe, for method): Lightly flour your bench and use a plastic bench scraper to release the dough from the bowl.

5. Gently press the dough to a rough oval. Fold the top third toward you and press lightly along the seam to adhere. Roll the dough over itself toward you again to create a log, using the the heel of your hand or your fingertips to seal the seam. Make sure your bench is lightly floured. You don't want too much pressure on the dough, but

neither do you want it to slide instead of roll. If the dough slides, brush away excess flour and wet your hands lightly.

6. Gently flip the dough so the seam is on the bottom, and use your hands to rock the ends of the loaf back and forth to create a football shape (bâtard). Then work your hands from the center of the loaf out toward the edges to elongate it slightly to 6 to 8 inches long. Transfer to a baking sheet lined with parchment paper.

7. Cover the dough with a towel and set it aside to proof for about 1 hour or until marshmallow-y in texture. If you poke the dough, it should spring back slightly, leaving an indent. Be careful not to over-proof, because you'll be cutting deeply into the loaf in the next step. After 30 minutes of proofing, preheat the oven to 450°F.

8. When the loaf is ready to bake, hold a lame at a 90-degree angle and cut a deep line (½ to 1 inch deep) down the center of the loaf, from one tapered end to the other. You may need to score and then score again to achieve this depth. Cut two additional lines to the same depth on either side of the center line, about an inch away. Cut two final lines on either side to the same depth. You should have five lines total.

9. Put the baking sheet in the oven, spritz the loaf with water 4 or 5 times, and close the door. Spray again after 3 minutes of baking, and again after another 3 minutes, working quickly to not lose oven heat. Bake for 20 to 25 minutes total until the loaf is a deep golden brown and the internal temperature registers about 190°F.

10. Transfer the loaf to a cooling rack for 15 to 20 minutes before cutting.

Pain de Mie

CHAPTER 4
BUTTERY AND AIRY

I've always been partial to enriched breads, and this chapter contains some of my favorites. The enriching elements in these loaves include milk, eggs, sugar, and/or butter, all of which result in a more tender, even crumb. We'll also take things up a notch with viennoiseries such as brioche and croissants. Viennoiseries (which translates to "things from Vienna") are the perfect cross between pastry and bread. They're yeast leavened but also include eggs, butter, cream, milk, and/or sugar, giving them a sweeter characteristic. They can also be laminated (as in the case of croissants).

We'll start this chapter with pain de mie, a light loaf perfect for sandwiches, traditionally baked in a Pullman loaf pan. Then we'll move into a soft, tender brioche. From there we move into le cramique, small raisin buns, and Viennoise au chocolat, which is dotted with dark chocolate chips. Lastly, we'll explore laminating dough by making classic croissants.

Savor each recipe in this chapter. They're so much fun to make and, of course, so much fun to eat!

Pain de Mie

Pain de mie is rumored to have been created to satisfy American and British tourists who found French breads too crusty and rustic. With its light, tender crumb (mie) and perfectly square shape, it is the ultimate sandwich loaf. This bread is traditionally baked in a Pullman loaf pan—which gives it its rectangular shape and has a lid to keep it from doming—but a traditional loaf pan topped with a sheet pan and a small weight on top before baking will achieve a similar effect.

Makes: 1 loaf

Prep time: **Active: 20 minutes; Inactive: 2 hours**

Bake time: **30 minutes**

Total time: **2 hours 50 minutes**

EQUIPMENT

• Medium bowl or stand mixer with dough hook

• Wooden spoon

• Linen towels or plastic wrap

• 1-pound Pullman loaf pan or 9-by-5-inch loaf pan

• Thermometer (optional)

• Cooling rack

⅓ cup (75 grams) whole milk

6 tablespoons (88 grams) water

Scant 2 teaspoons (5 grams) instant yeast

2⅔ cups (312 grams) all-purpose flour (or T55 flour), plus more for shaping

2 tablespoons (25 grams) granulated sugar

2 teaspoons (6 grams) kosher salt

2½ tablespoons (40 grams) crème fraîche

Butter or nonstick spray, for greasing

1. Make the dough: In a medium bowl, stir together the milk, water, and yeast. Add the flour, sugar, salt, and crème fraîche, and stir until a shaggy dough comes together. Turn the dough onto a clean bench and knead for 8 to 10 minutes (or transfer to a stand mixer and knead for 6 to 8 minutes at low speed) until smooth, stretchy, and supple.

2. If kneading by hand, return the dough to the bowl. Cover with a towel and set aside for 1 to 1½ hours at room temperature. The dough should double in size. (This timing will vary, depending on your kitchen temperature.) Lightly grease a loaf pan.

3. Shape and bake: Turn the dough out onto a lightly floured bench and gently press into a 9-inch square. Fold in the sides to meet the center, then roll the dough up in the opposite direction, starting at one short end and ending at the other, to form a rolled log. Lightly roll with your hands to lengthen the log to 9 inches.

4. Transfer to the loaf pan seam-side down, cover with a towel, and set aside to proof for about 1 hour, until marshmallow-y in texture and about ½ inch from the top of the pan. If you poke the dough, it should spring back slightly, leaving an indent.

5. After 30 minutes of proofing, preheat the oven to 375°F.

6. Put the lid on the pan (optional). Transfer the pan to the oven and bake for 25 minutes.

7. Remove the lid (if using) and continue baking for an additional 5 to 10 minutes, or until the loaf is a deep golden brown and a thermometer inserted into the center registers about 200°F.

8. Immediately turn the loaf out onto a cooling rack and let it sit for 15 to 20 minutes before slicing.

Ingredient tip: The crème fraîche in this recipe not only gives the bread a rich texture but also adds a touch of tanginess. If you don't have any, you can use room-temperature unsalted butter instead.

Brioche

Brioche is the perfect blend of bread and pastry. With its high fat content, brioche was once considered a great luxury. In fact, Marie Antoinette's famous utterance, "Let them eat cake," was "Qu'ils mangent de la brioche" (though she may not have said either phrase). Brioche likely originated in Normandy in the early 15th century, and the lighter, fluffier version that we know today was popularized in the 18th century. Its buttery, feathery texture makes it ideal for just about any occasion.

Makes: 1 loaf

Prep time: **Active: 35 minutes; Inactive: 4 hours 30 minutes**

Bake time: 30 minutes

Total time: 5 hours 35 minutes

EQUIPMENT

• Medium bowl or stand mixer with dough hook

• Wooden spoon

• Rubber spatula (optional)

• Linen towel or plastic wrap

• Plastic bench scraper

• Kitchen scale (optional)

• 9-by-5-inch loaf pan

• Whisk or fork

• Pastry brush

• Thermometer (optional)

• Cooling rack

¼ cup (60 grams) whole milk

2 teaspoons (6 grams) instant yeast

4 (200 grams) large eggs, divided

2⅔ cups (325 grams) bread flour (or T55 flour), plus more for shaping

3 tablespoons (40 grams) granulated sugar

2 teaspoons (6 grams) kosher salt

⅔ cup (150 grams) unsalted butter, at room temperature (65 to 70°F), plus more for greasing

1. Make the dough: In a medium bowl, lightly stir together the milk, yeast, and 3 (150 grams) eggs. Add the flour, sugar, and salt, and stir until a shaggy dough comes together. Turn the dough onto a clean bench and knead for 6 to 8 minutes (or transfer to a stand mixer and knead for 4 to 5 minutes at low speed) until smooth. Return the dough to the bowl and mix in the butter a bit at a time, either by hand or with the dough hook, and continue to knead until the butter is well incorporated. You may need to scrape down the bowl with a spatula occasionally while kneading.

2. Cover with a towel and set aside for 1 to 1½ hours at room temperature. The dough should double in size. (This timing will vary, depending on your kitchen temperature.)

3. Shape and bake: Transfer the bowl to the refrigerator for at least 2 hours (overnight if possible) before shaping. The colder the dough (and the fat within the dough), the easier and less sticky it will be to work with.

4. Once the dough is cold, use a bench scraper to evenly divide it into 6 equal pieces, using a scale if you have one (photos A and B). Sprinkle the top of each piece lightly with flour.

5. Gently flatten one dough piece, then use your fingertips to pull the edges of the dough into the center and pinch to shape it into a rough round (photo C). Flip the round over. Cup the dough in your hand and, using the grip of your bench, rotate the round against the table to tighten the seam (photo D). Dust the top with flour if necessary to prevent it from sticking to your hand. Work quickly to avoid the fat warming too fast. Repeat with the remaining rounds.

D

6. Grease a loaf pan with butter. Transfer the rounds to the pan seam-side down, lining them up two by two. Cover with a towel and set aside for 1½ to 2 hours, until marshmallow-y in texture and doubled in volume (photo E). If you poke the dough, it should spring back slightly, leaving an indent. After 1 hour of proofing, preheat the oven to 375°F.

E

7. Whisk the remaining 1 (50 grams) egg with a splash of water and gently brush this glaze over the loaf.

8. Bake for 30 to 35 minutes, until the loaf is golden brown and a thermometer inserted into the center registers about 200°F.

9. Immediately turn the loaf out onto a cooling rack, turn right-side up, and let it sit for 15 to 20 minutes before slicing.

Variation tip: Brioche is one of the most versatile doughs. It can be easily transformed into classic brioche à tête—the little, individual loaves baked in fluted tins with little balls, or "heads," on their peaks—or Tarte Tropézienne, a round, flat loaf cut in half and filled with a layer of pastry cream. You can use a muffin tin for baking the former, and a baking sheet for the latter. You can even use brioche to make the most-over-the-top doughnuts, cinnamon buns, hamburger buns, and more.

Le Cramique

These rich, sweet buns brimming with plump raisins are made with a dough and a method similar to brioche. Le cramique (kramiek in Flemish) originated as early as the 13th century in Belgium and later developed into cramiche in France, a name that combines the words crème (cream) and miche (loaf).

Makes: 14 buns

Prep time: Active: 35 minutes; Inactive: 4 hours 30 minutes

Bake time: 20 minutes

Total time: 5 hours 25 minutes

EQUIPMENT
- Medium bowl or stand mixer with dough hook
- Wooden spoon
- Rubber spatula (optional)
- Linen towel or plastic wrap
- 2 heavy baking sheets
- Parchment paper
- Metal bench scraper
- Kitchen scale (optional)
- Whisk
- Pastry brush
- Kitchen shears

¾ cup (175 grams) whole milk

2 teaspoons (6 grams) instant yeast

3 (150 grams) large eggs, divided

4⅛ cups (500 grams) bread flour (or T55 flour), plus more for shaping

3 tablespoons (40 grams) granulated sugar

1 tablespoon (9 grams) kosher salt

9 tablespoons (125 grams) unsalted butter, at room temperature (65 to 70°F)

⅔ cup (100 grams) dark raisins, soaked in ⅔ cup (150 grams) warm water for at least 1 hour or overnight

¼ cup (50 grams) pearl sugar (optional)

1. Make the dough: In a medium bowl, lightly stir together the milk, yeast, and 2 (100 grams) eggs. Add the flour, sugar, and salt, and stir until a shaggy dough comes together. Turn the dough onto a clean bench and knead for 6 to 8 minutes (or transfer to a stand mixer and knead for 4 to 5 minutes at low speed) until smooth. Return the dough to the bowl and mix in the butter a bit at a time, either by hand or with the dough hook, and continue to knead until the butter is well incorporated. You may need to scrape down the bowl with a spatula occasionally while kneading.

2. Cover with a towel and set aside for 1 to 1½ hours at room temperature. The dough should double in size. (This timing will vary, depending on your kitchen temperature.)

3. Transfer the bowl to the refrigerator for at least 2 hours and up to overnight. The colder the dough, the easier and less sticky it will be to work with.

4. Line two baking sheets with parchment paper. Once the dough is cold, lightly flour your bench and press the dough out to a ½-inch-thick rectangle. Strain the raisins and transfer to a paper towel to dry for 2 minutes, then spread them evenly over the dough, pressing lightly to adhere. Fold the dough in half to enclose the raisins.

5. Evenly divide the dough into 14 pieces with a metal bench scraper, ideally by using a scale. Sprinkle the top of each piece lightly with flour.

6. Shape and bake: On a clean bench, gently flatten a piece of dough, then use your fingertips to pull the corners of the dough into the center and pinch to shape into a rough round (see step-by-step

photos in the brioche recipe, for method). Flip the round over. Cup the dough within your hand and, using the grip of your bench, rotate to tighten the seam. Dust the top with flour if necessary to prevent it from sticking to your hand. Work quickly to avoid the fat warming too fast. Repeat with the remaining rounds.

7. Transfer the buns to the prepared baking sheets seam-side down, spacing them at least 3 inches apart. Cover with a towel and set aside for 1 to 1½ hours, until marshmallow-y in texture. If you poke the dough, it should spring back slightly, leaving an indent. After 45 minutes of proofing, preheat the oven to 400°F.

8. Whisk the remaining 1 egg (50 grams) with a splash of water and use a pastry brush to gently brush this glaze over each bun. Use kitchen shears to snip the top of each round to create an X. Fill each X with a sprinkle of pearl sugar (if using).

9. Bake the buns for 20 to 24 minutes, until they are golden brown. Serve warm.

Variation tip: This bread can also be baked on a baking sheet or in a loaf pan and served in slices. Use the same technique as for Pain de Mie to shape the dough for a loaf, or shape into a large round using the same technique as for Boule de Pain.

Viennoise au Chocolat

Viennoise au chocolat is deceptively simple to make. The enriched dough is smooth and very forgiving. Because it's so easy to handle, it offers a great opportunity to practice kneading dough to the proper consistency, shaping, proofing while using a couche, scoring, and more. And, of course, the final result has a decadent and irresistible rich, soft texture.

Makes: 3 loaves

Prep time: Active: 30 minutes; Inactive: 3 hours 30 minutes

Bake time: 20 minutes

Total time: 4 hours 20 minutes

EQUIPMENT
- Medium bowl or stand mixer with dough hook
- Wooden spoon
- Linen towel or plastic wrap
- Bench scrapers (plastic and metal)
- Kitchen scale (optional)
- Couche (or another linen towel)
- Heavy baking sheet
- Parchment paper
- Whisk
- Pastry brush
- Lame or razor
- Thermometer (optional)
- Cooling rack

¾ cup plus 2 tablespoons (200 grams) whole milk

2 teaspoons (6 grams) instant yeast

4⅛ cup (500 grams) bread flour (or T55 flour)

3 tablespoons (40 grams) granulated sugar

1 tablespoon (9 grams) kosher salt

4½ tablespoons (65 grams) unsalted butter

½ cup (85 grams) dark chocolate chips

1 (50 grams) large egg

1. Make the dough: In a medium bowl, stir together the milk and yeast. Add the flour, sugar, salt, and butter, and stir until a shaggy dough comes together. Turn the dough onto your bench and knead for 8 to 10 minutes (or transfer to a stand mixer and knead for 6 to 8 minutes at low speed) until smooth.

2. If kneading by hand, return the dough to the bowl. Cover with a towel and set aside for 1 to 1½ hours at room temperature. The dough should double in size. (This timing will vary, depending on your kitchen temperature.)

3. Transfer the bowl to the refrigerator for 1 to 2 hours (overnight if possible) before shaping. The colder the dough (and the fat within the dough), the easier and less sticky it will be to work with.

4. Shape and bake (see step-by-step photos in the pain complet recipe, for method): Lightly flour your bench and use a plastic bench scraper to release the dough from the bowl. Use a metal bench scraper to portion the dough into 3 equal sections, ideally using a scale.

5. Using your fingertips, gently press a piece of dough into a rough rectangle. Sprinkle the dough with one-third of the chocolate chips, pressing them to adhere. Fold the top third of the dough toward you and press lightly along the seam to adhere. Fold the top half of the dough over the bottom half to create a log. Use the heel of your hand or your fingertips to seal the seam. Make sure your bench is lightly floured. You don't want too much pressure on the dough, but nor do you want it to slide instead of roll. If the dough slides, brush away excess flour and wet your hands lightly.

6. Gently flip the dough so the seam is on the bottom, and use your hands to rock the ends of the loaf back and forth to create a football shape. Then work your hands from the center of the loaf out toward the edges to elongate it to about 12 inches long. Repeat with the remaining pieces of dough.

7. Lay a couche or a linen towel on a baking sheet and fold one end to create a border. Place one loaf next to this fold. Fold it along the other side to create a dedicated space for the loaf to rise. Lay a loaf alongside and create another fold. Repeat once more. Cover with a towel and set aside to proof for 1 hour or until marshmallow-y in texture. If you poke the dough, it should spring back slightly, leaving an indent.

8. After 30 minutes of proofing, preheat the oven to 425°F. Line a baking sheet with parchment paper.

9. When the loaves are ready to bake, gently lift and transfer each loaf to the prepared baking sheet, placing them a few inches apart.

10. In a small bowl, whisk the egg with a splash of water, and use a pastry brush to brush this glaze over the loaves. Hold a lame at a 30-degree angle, and quickly and lightly score 8 to 10½-inch-deep lines spaced 1 inch apart diagonally across the top of each loaf. Between loaves, dip the lame into water to release any sticky bits of dough.

11. Put the baking sheet in the oven. Bake for 18 to 20 minutes, until the loaves are deep golden brown and a thermometer inserted into the center registers about 200°F.

12. Transfer the loaves to a cooling rack or serve warm.

Croissants

Buttery, flaky croissants are the quintessential viennoiserie and a symbol of France (even though they were originally Austrian). The layers of fat in this dough create steam when baking, and the combination of steam and yeast creates the light and airy texture croissants are known for, as well as the flaky, crisp exterior. The dough must be chilled before being baked —the cold butter creates those flaky layers. If the butter and dough become warm, the dough will absorb the fat, leaving you with more of a biscuit than a croissant. Don't rush croissants—under-proofed croissants will have gummy centers. And make sure you use your ruler to measure the size of the dough and butter you're rolling—it must be exact.

Makes: 10

Prep time: Active: 1 hour 30 minutes; Inactive: 5 hours

Bake time: 30 minutes

Total time: 7 hours

EQUIPMENT
- Medium bowl or stand mixer with dough hook
- Wooden spoon
- Linen towel
- Parchment paper
- Rolling pin
- Plastic bench scraper
- Ruler
- Plastic wrap
- Heavy baking sheet
- Paring knife
- Chef's knife or pizza cutter
- Whisk
- Pastry brush

¾ cup plus 1 tablespoon (180 grams) whole milk

2 teaspoons (6 grams) instant yeast

2⅔ cups (312 grams) all-purpose flour (or T55 flour), plus extra for shaping

1 tablespoon plus 1½ teaspoons (20 grams) granulated sugar

2 teaspoons (6 grams) kosher salt

1 cup (225 grams) unsalted butter, at room temperature (65 to 70°F), divided

1 (50 grams) large egg

1. Make the dough: In a medium bowl, stir together the milk and yeast, then add the flour, sugar, salt, and butter and stir until a shaggy dough forms. Turn the dough out onto a clean bench and knead for 8 to 10 minutes (or transfer to a stand mixer and knead for 6 to 8 minutes at low speed) until smooth, stretchy, and supple.

2. If kneading by hand, return the dough to the bowl. Cover with a towel and set aside for 1 hour or until doubled in size. (This timing will vary, depending on your kitchen temperature.)

3. Turn the dough out onto a clean bench and press lightly to an 8-inch square. Wrap with plastic wrap and refrigerate for 1 hour. This is known as the dough block (détrempe). The dough block and butter block should have a similar temperature and consistency, so chilling is essential.

4. After 30 minutes of chilling the dough block, place the remaining ¾ cup (170 grams) of butter on a piece of parchment paper. Top with an additional sheet of parchment paper and use a rolling pin and plastic bench scraper to shape the butter into a 6-by-8-inch rectangle. Slide the packet of parchment paper onto a baking sheet and transfer to the refrigerator for 15 to 20 minutes, until firm but pliable. You should be able to bend the packet without it snapping into shards.

5. Set the butter block aside on your bench while you shape the dough. This will ensure that it's the correct temperature (not too cold) before incorporation. Dust your bench and the top of the dough with flour and roll the dough block into a 9-by-13-inch rectangle. Brush off excess flour. Unwrap the butter and flip it onto the center of the dough, so its edges almost meet the sides of the dough block (photo A). Fold the top and bottom portions of dough over the butter block, meeting in the center. Thoroughly pinch the center and end seams closed (photo B). Temperature is crucial, so work quickly.

A

6. Dust your bench with flour and rotate the dough so the center seam is pointing toward you. Roll the dough out, using a back-and-forth motion, to create a 7-by-21-inch rectangle, working carefully so no butter escapes from the dough (photo C). If butter peeks through, pinch the dough around it to cover and dust with flour. Brush off excess flour before folding.

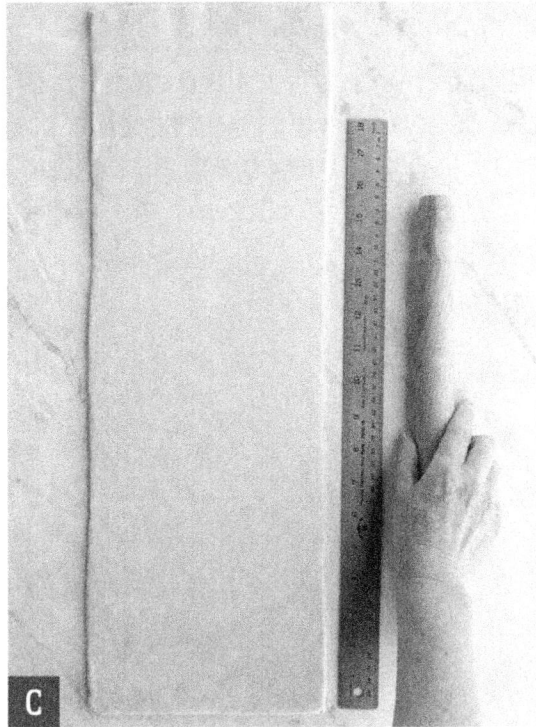

7. Fold the top third of the dough toward the center, then fold the bottom third of the dough over the center to create a letter fold (photo D). Brush off excess flour.

8. Wrap the dough in plastic wrap and chill for 30 minutes.

9. Repeat step 6, starting with the folded edge of the dough on your left side, rolling the dough into a 7-by-21-inch rectangle, and creating a letter fold (photo E). Wrap the dough again and chill for 45 minutes.

10. Repeat this step once more, then wrap the dough and chill for at least 1 hour or overnight.

11. Shape and bake: Line a baking sheet with parchment paper.

12. Dust your bench with flour and roll the dough into a ¼-inch-thick rectangle, about 9 by 20 inches (similar to photo C). Use a paring knife to mark 4-inch sections along the length of the long side. Use a chef's knife to cut the rectangle at the 4-inch marks, creating five 4-by-9-inch sections (photo F). Halve each of these sections diagonally to create a total of 10 triangles (photo G).

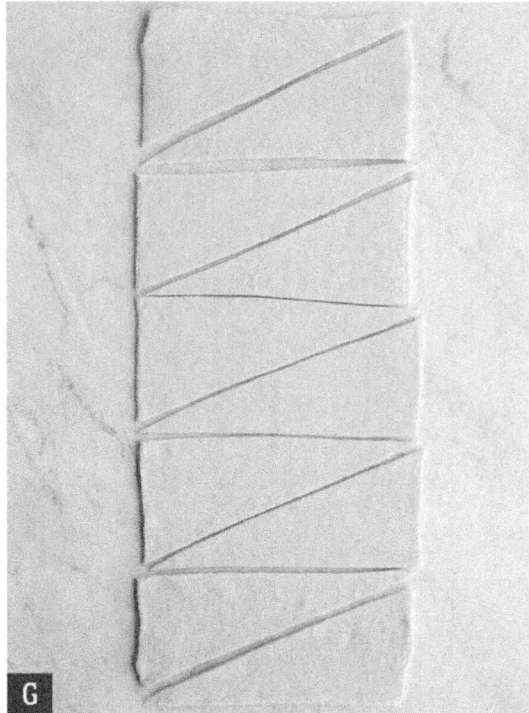

G

13. Stretch the bottom of each triangle lightly to elongate it a bit. Starting on the long side, roll the triangles to create a croissant shape (photos H and I). When you've almost reached the end of the roll, pull the tip a bit to elongate it and wrap it around the croissant, pinching lightly to seal. Place each croissant on the prepared baking sheet with the tips on the bottom to keep them from opening while proofing and baking. Space them a few inches apart.

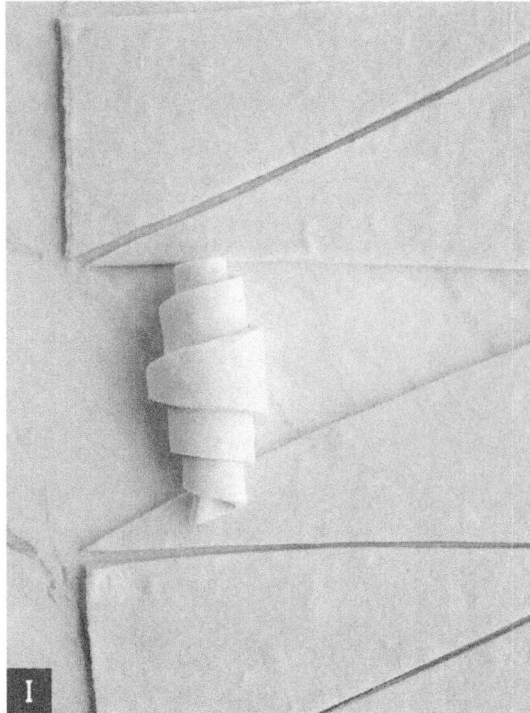

14. Cover the tray with plastic wrap and set aside to proof at room temperature for 1½ to 2½ hours. (This timing will vary, depending on your kitchen temperature, but the ideal temperature is 75°F to 80°F.) Proof until it reaches a marshmallow-y consistency and an increase in volume. If you poke the dough, it should spring back slightly, leaving an indent.

15. After 1 hour of proofing, preheat the oven to 400°F.

16. In a small bowl, whisk the egg with a splash of water and use a pastry brush to brush the glaze over the croissants. Brush them once more, for extra shine.

17. Bake for 30 to 35 minutes until the croissants are a deep golden brown. Serve warm.

Baking tip: If the heat of your oven tends to brown the bottom of your baked goods too quickly, double up the baking sheets when baking croissants.

Variation tip: Once prepared, this dough can be filled with chocolate batons or a line of chocolate chips before the croissants are rolled up to create pain au chocolat, or strips of ham and cheese for delicious savory croissants, among countless other flavor ideas.

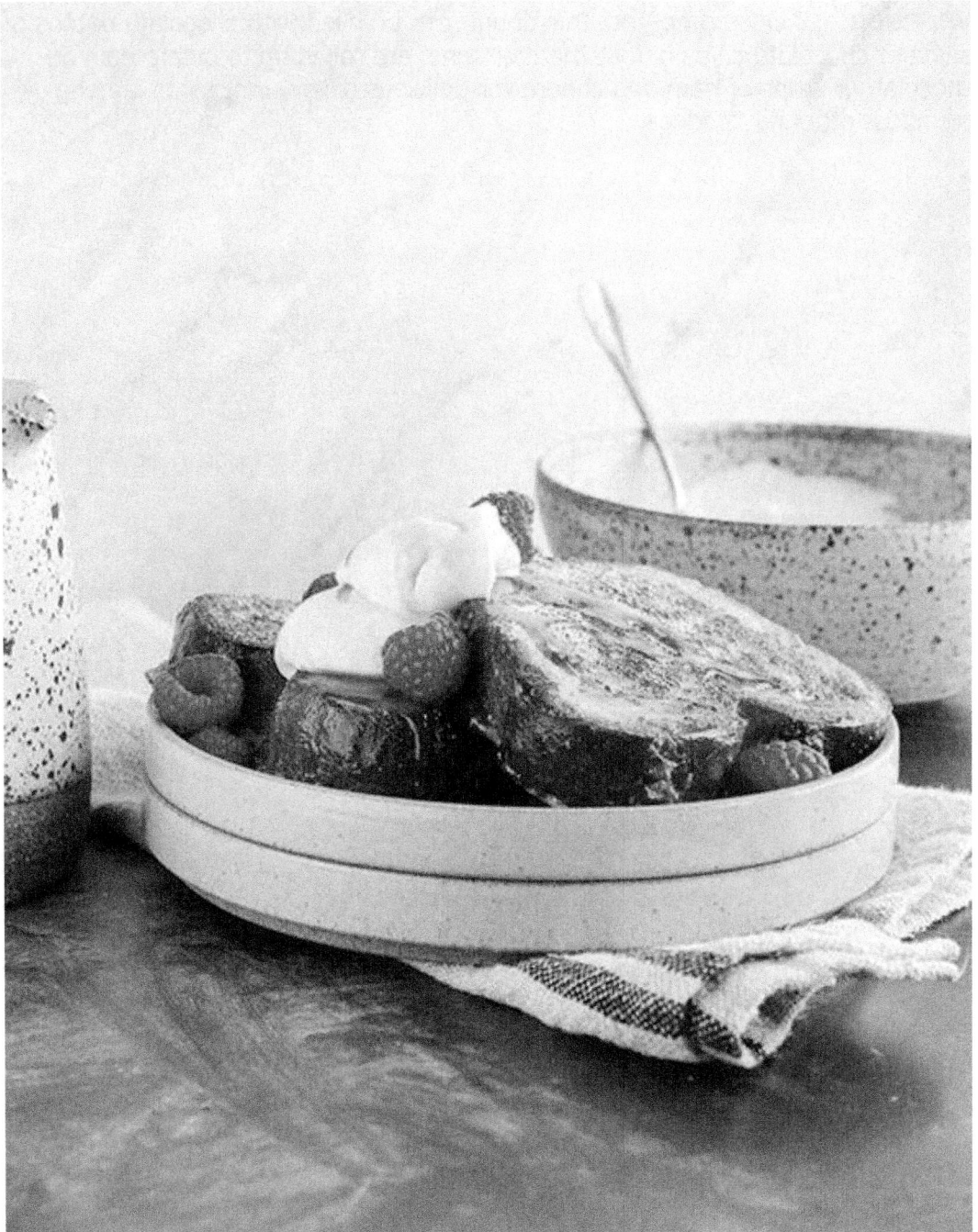

Pain Perdu with Whipped Crème Fraîche

CHAPTER 5

BEYOND BREAD

Pain Perdu with Whipped Crème Fraîche
Bourbon Chocolate Croissant Bread Pudding
Everyday Bread Salad
French Onion Soup
Tartines

As the old saying goes, man cannot live on bread alone. If you're anything like me, you've been eating what you could the day and the day after these loaves were baked but sensibly stockpiled the rest in your freezer to enjoy later. Well, now is the time to break out those loaves and whip up a fantastic meal!

We start with a pain perdu made with buttery brioche (and baked so that it puffs up), and a bread pudding made with croissants and chocolate for a light, fluffy texture. Then we have the savory dishes: a salad that combines pieces of boule with bright, flavorful vegetables; a classic French onion soup; and, last but not least, three different open-faced tartine sandwiches. The recipes in this chapter are some of my favorite ways to use up leftover bread. And while it wasn't done purposely, all five items placed on a table together make up an absolutely perfect brunch.

Pain Perdu with Whipped Crème Fraîche

Pain perdu, or "lost bread," has been enjoyed for centuries, dating back to the Roman Empire. Like diner-style French toast, it's soaked generously with custard, but then it is baked to ensure that the interior stays fluffy. And don't skimp on the whipped crème fraîche! The tanginess takes it to the next level, and it cuts into the baked bread's nutty sweetness perfectly.

Makes: 4 servings
Prep time: 40 minutes
Bake time: 5 minutes
Total time: 45 minutes

FOR THE WHIPPED CRÈME FRAÎCHE
1 cup heavy (whipping) cream
¼ cup crème fraîche
3 to 4 tablespoons confectioners' sugar
1 teaspoon pure vanilla extract
¼ teaspoon kosher salt
1 teaspoon grated lemon zest (optional)

FOR THE PAIN PERDU
1 cup half-and-half (or whole milk)
4 large eggs
1 teaspoon pure vanilla extract
2 tablespoons granulated sugar
½ teaspoon ground cinnamon
½ teaspoon kosher salt
⅛ teaspoon ground nutmeg (optional)
1 loaf Brioche, ends trimmed, cut into 1-inch-thick slices

4 tablespoons (56 grams) unsalted butter

1 cup fresh raspberries

1 cup maple syrup

Confectioners' sugar, for dusting (optional)

1. Preheat the oven to 425°F. Line a baking sheet with parchment paper.

2. Make the whipped crème fraîche: In a medium bowl or the bowl of a stand mixer fitted with a whisk attachment, whip the cream on medium speed until soft peaks form. Add the crème fraîche, sugar, vanilla, salt, and lemon zest (if using). Whip to medium peaks (when lifting the whisk upside down, the cream should look like a hook), cover the bowl with plastic wrap, and refrigerate.

3. Make the pain perdu: In a medium bowl, whisk together the half-and-half, eggs, vanilla, sugar, cinnamon, salt, and nutmeg (if using).

4. Working with one brioche slice at a time, dip the bread into the egg mixture and let soak for 1 minute.

5. In a medium sauté pan over medium-low heat, melt 1 tablespoon of butter until sizzling lightly.

6. Flip the brioche and soak for 30 additional seconds, then transfer to the pan. Continue soaking slices as you cook.

7. Cook each piece of brioche until browned on the bottom, 1 to 2 minutes, then flip and cook for an additional minute before transferring to the prepared baking sheet. Repeat with the remaining slices, adding a tablespoon of butter to the pan as needed.

8. Bake for 4 to 5 minutes, until the centers spring back when poked. Serve warm with whipped crème fraîche, raspberries, and maple syrup. Dust with confectioners' sugar, if desired.

Bourbon Chocolate Croissant Bread Pudding

Years ago, when I first started selling croissants in my bakery, I always ended up with leftovers. One day, I mixed up a batch of bread pudding, threw in some chocolate chips, and hoped for the best. It was an instant hit. I kept making it, and it always sold out. This isn't a typical mushy bread pudding; you should see chunks of gorgeous croissant in every bite, lightly sweetened with the baked custard soaking in.

Serves 9
Prep time: 15 minutes
Bake time: 20 minutes
Total time: 35 minutes

1½ cups half-and-half
3 large eggs
⅔ cup plus 1 tablespoon granulated sugar, divided
½ teaspoon ground cinnamon
¾ teaspoon kosher salt
2 tablespoons bourbon
9 Croissants, cut into 1-inch cubes
½ cup dark chocolate chips
¼ cup confectioners' sugar (optional)

1. Preheat the oven to 425°F. Line an 8- or 9-inch square baking pan with parchment paper or spray with nonstick baking spray.

2. In a large bowl, whisk together the half-and-half, eggs, ⅔ cup of granulated sugar, the cinnamon, and salt. Whisk in the bourbon.

3. Add the croissant cubes and toss lightly with a rubber spatula or spoon to coat the cubes (don't mash them!). Set aside for 2 to 3

minutes, to let the liquid absorb into the bread, then add the chocolate chips and lightly toss again.

4. Pour the mixture into the prepared baking pan and gently press with a spatula to spread it evenly. Sprinkle with the remaining 1 tablespoon of granulated sugar.

5. Bake for 18 to 22 minutes until the bread pudding is golden brown. Cut into 9 squares. Serve warm, dusted with confectioners' sugar (if using) or additional melted chocolate, if desired, to take things over the top.

Variation tip: If you can't part ways with your croissants, feel free to substitute cubes of brioche.

Everyday Bread Salad

I call this recipe an *"everyday"* dish, but this salad is good for just about any occasion, whether it's a summer barbecue, fancy dinner party, or casual brunch. I love this combo as written, but feel free to incorporate capers, olives, cheeses, or crisped prosciutto. You can even add roast chicken to transform it into a hearty main course.

Serves 4 to 6
Prep time: 25 minutes
Bake time: 6 minutes
Total time: 31 minutes

½ loaf <u>boule de pain</u>, cut into 1-inch cubes
½ cup plus 2 tablespoons olive oil, divided
1 teaspoon kosher salt, divided
2 teaspoons minced garlic
1 tablespoon minced shallot
2 tablespoons white wine vinegar
½ teaspoon freshly ground black pepper
2 pints cherry tomatoes, halved
1 medium cucumber, seeded and thinly sliced
½ small red onion, thinly sliced
¼ cup roughly chopped fresh basil leaves
1 cup crumbled feta

1. Preheat the oven to 450°F. Line a baking sheet with parchment paper.

2. Pour the bread cubes onto the prepared baking sheet and toss with 2 tablespoons of oil and ½ teaspoon of salt. Bake for 6 to 8 minutes,

until lightly browned along the edges. Add the garlic, toss with a rubber spatula, and return to the oven for 2 to 3 minutes, until the bread is crisp but chewy. Remove and set aside to cool slightly.

3. In a large bowl, whisk together the shallot, vinegar, remaining ½ teaspoon of salt, and the pepper. While whisking constantly, slowly pour in the remaining ½ cup of oil in a steady stream.

4. Add the tomatoes, cucumber, and red onion to the bowl and toss to coat with the dressing. Pour in the bread cubes and toss to coat. Add the basil and cheese (if using), and lightly toss. Serve immediately or refrigerate for up to 1 hour to allow the flavors to develop and the bread to soak up more vinaigrette.

Variation tip: A classic French vinaigrette would include a bit of Dijon mustard, so feel free to whisk in 1 or 2 teaspoons. You can also use goat cheese or small balls of mozzarella in place of the feta.

French Onion Soup

French onion soup is a revelation.I promise you1l get through slicing those onions,and once you taste that first spoonful,with that perfectly soaked baguette crouton dripping with Gruyère cheese,it1l all be worth it.

Serves 6

Prep time: **Active: 50 minutes; Inactive: 50 minutes**

Bake time: **7 minutes**

Total time: **1 hour 47 minutes**

4 tablespoons olive oil, divided

4 tablespoons unsalted butter

6 (3 pounds) yellow onions, thinly sliced

2 tablespoons minced garlic

½ cup dry sherry or white wine

2 quarts beef stock

2 teaspoons kosher salt

¾ teaspoon freshly ground black pepper

6 thyme sprigs, plus more for serving

1 baguette, sliced diagonally into 12½-inch-thick slices (keep any extras for dunking)

8 ounces Gruyère cheese, shredded, divided

1. In a Dutch oven or a large, heavy-bottomed pot, combine 2 tablespoons of oil with the butter and heat over medium heat until the butter begins to sizzle. Add the onions, stirring to coat them with fat. Cook over low to medium heat, stirring every 5 minutes, for

45 to 60 minutes, until the onions are a deep golden brown. During the last few minutes of cooking, stir in the garlic.

2. Add the sherry and stir to deglaze the pan, scraping up any bits from the bottom of the pot. Continue to cook over medium heat, stirring, until the liquid has evaporated. Add the stock, salt, pepper, and thyme and bring to a boil. Simmer over low to medium heat for 20 to 30 minutes until the soup has deepened slightly in color and flavor. Taste and adjust the seasoning as desired, then remove from the heat and remove the thyme.

3. Preheat the oven to 425°F. Line a baking sheet with parchment paper. Place the baguette slices on the prepared baking sheet. Drizzle or brush with the remaining oil, and toast until lightly browned along the edges, 4 to 6 minutes.

4. Remove from the oven. Turn on the broiler. Top 12 baguette slices with half of the Gruyère cheese. Broil for 2 minutes until melted and browned in spots.

5. Ladle hot soup into 6 bowls, and sprinkle evenly with the remaining Gruyère cheese. Top each bowl with 2 toasts and a small thyme sprig.

Tartines

It's said that open-faced sandwiches were introduced during the Middle Ages as a way for people to enjoy a meal without plates or utensils. Today, tartines are a popular breakfast. But tartines are eaten all day long; after all, a perfectly toasted slice of hearty bread is the ultimate canvas.

Makes: 4 of each type
Prep time: 5 to 40 minutes
Total time: 10 to 50 minutes

FOR ALL TARTINES
Pain de Campagne, cut into ½-inch-thick slices
Olive oil, for brushing

FOR SMOKED SALMON TARTINES
½ cup cream cheese or crème fraîche
8 ounces smoked salmon
¼ red onion, thinly sliced
Fresh dill sprigs or capers (optional)
1 lemon, cut into wedges

FOR FIG AND GOAT CHEESE TARTINES
½ cup black currant or fig jam (optional)
6 ounces herbed goat cheese
6 to 8 fresh figs, halved
½ cup toasted walnuts, roughly chopped
Balsamic vinegar, for drizzling
Honey, for drizzling
4 thyme sprigs (or ½ cup arugula)

FOR TURKEY TARTINES

Bacon jam, apple butter, or Dijon mustard

4 ounces Brie cheese, sliced

6 ounces sliced deli or roasted turkey

1 Pink Lady or Honeycrisp apple, cored and thinly sliced

TO TOAST THE BREAD:

Preheat the oven to 450°F. Put bread slices on a baking sheet, brush with oil, and bake for 4 to 5 minutes until lightly crisped along the edges.

TO ASSEMBLE THE SMOKED SALMON TARTINES:

Slather the toasts with cream cheese and top with smoked salmon, red onion, and capers or dill (if using). Serve with lemon wedges.

TO ASSEMBLE THE FIG AND GOAT CHEESE TARTINES:

If using, spread a thin layer of jam over the toasts. Top with cheese, fig halves, and walnuts. Drizzle with balsamic vinegar and honey, and garnish with thyme.

TO ASSEMBLE THE TURKEY TARTINES:

Spread a thin layer of bacon jam or other topping over the toasts. Top with Brie, turkey, and apple.

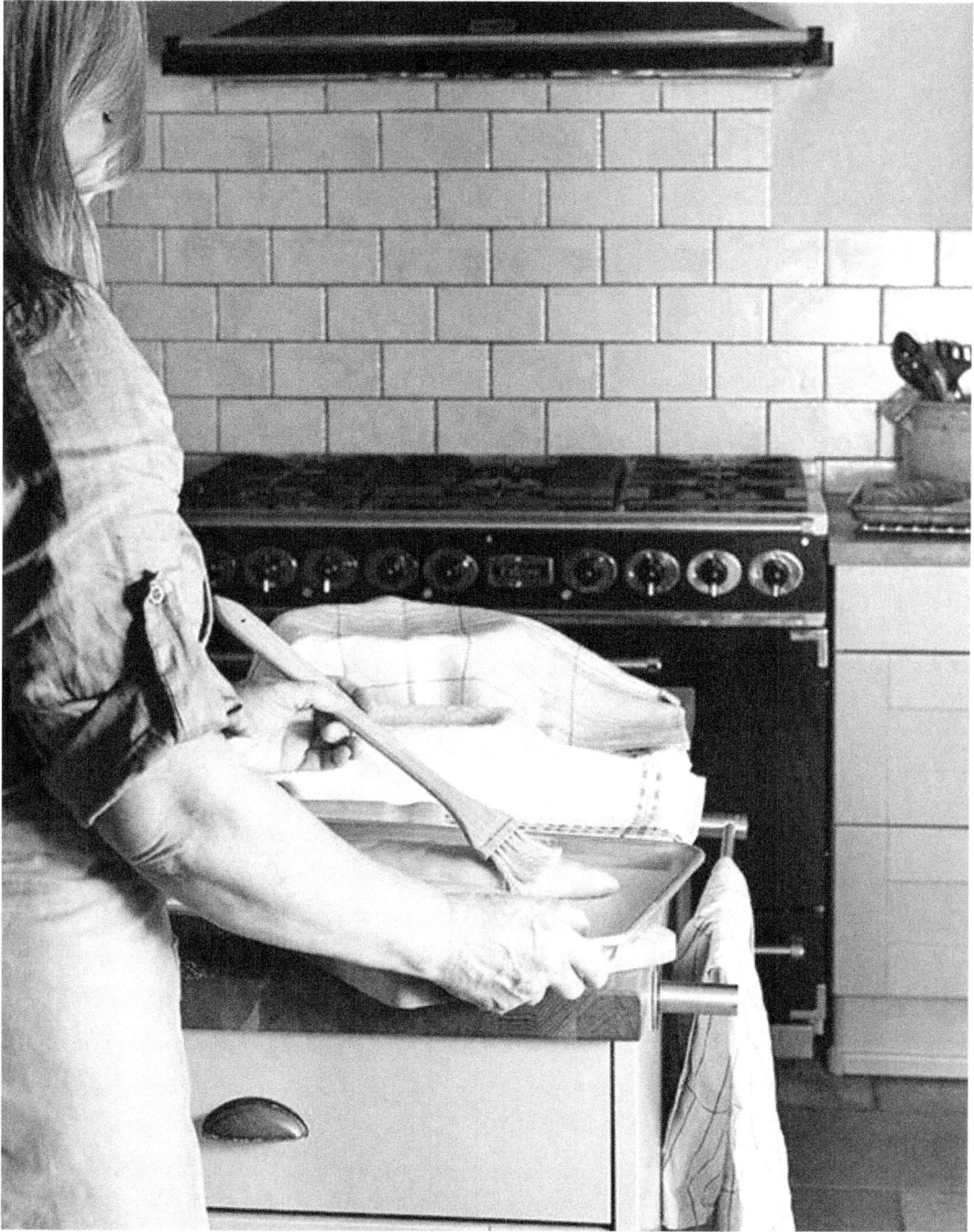

MEASUREMENT CONVERSIONS

VOLUME EQUIVALENTS	U.S. STANDARD	U.S. STANDARD (OUNCES)	METRIC (APPROXIMATE)
LIQUID	2 tablespoons	1 fl. oz.	30 mL
	¼ cup	2 fl. oz.	60 mL
	½ cup	4 fl. oz.	120 mL
	1 cup	8 fl. oz.	240 mL
	1½ cups	12 fl. oz.	355 mL
	2 cups or 1 pint	16 fl. oz.	475 mL
	4 cups or 1 quart	32 fl. oz.	1 L
	1 gallon	128 fl. oz.	4 L
DRY	⅛ teaspoon	—	0.5 mL
	¼ teaspoon	—	1 mL
	½ teaspoon	—	2 mL
	¾ teaspoon	—	4 mL
	1 teaspoon	—	5 mL
	1 tablespoon	—	15 mL
	¼ cup	—	59 mL
	⅓ cup	—	79 mL
	½ cup	—	118 mL
	⅔ cup	—	156 mL
	¾ cup	—	177 mL
	1 cup	—	235 mL
	2 cups or 1 pint	—	475 mL
	3 cups	—	700 mL
	4 cups or 1 quart	—	1 L
	½ gallon	—	2 L
	1 gallon	—	4 L

OVEN TEMPERATURES

FAHRENHEIT	CELSIUS (APPROXIMATE)
250°F	120°C
300°F	150°C
325°F	165°C
350°F	180°C
375°F	190°C
400°F	200°C
425°F	220°C
450°F	230°C

WEIGHT EQUIVALENTS

U.S. STANDARD	METRIC (APPROXIMATE)
½ ounce	15 g
1 ounce	30 g
2 ounces	60 g
4 ounces	115 g
8 ounces	225 g
12 ounces	340 g
16 ounces or 1 pound	455 g

Printed in Great Britain
by Amazon